RAMMED EARTH STRU

A code of practice

Rammed Earth Structures

A code of practice

JULIAN KEABLE

INTERMEDIATE TECHNOLOGY PUBLICATIONS 1996

Published by Intermediate Technology Publications Ltd
103-105 Southampton Row, London WC1 4HH, UK

ODA This book was produced by Julian Keable, funded by the
Overseas Development Administration of the United Kingdom.
However, the Overseas Development Administration can accept
no responsibility for any information provided or views expressed. The book
results from a project initiated by Urbanaid Africa, and completed by the
Executive Consultant Julian Keable of Julian Keable and Partners, together with
the consultant team. Consultant Advisors were John Norton of Development
Workshop; Robin Spence of Cambridge Architectural Research Ltd; and
Graham Tipple of the Centre for Architectural Research and Development
Overseas. Associated research institutions were the Department of Civil
Engineering, University of Newcastle-upon-Tyne; Natural Resources Institute,
ODA, Chatham; and the Department of Biology, Queen Mary College, London.

The drawings are by Adam Brockbank, London

ISBN 1 85339 350 9

Typeset by Diamond People Ltd., Bromyard
Printed in UK by SRP, Exeter

Contents

Tests

Ramming in progress (formwork used as scaffold)

INTRODUCTION

Rammed earth structures

Ramming earth has been a method of construction used for centuries in various parts of the world, and is commonly known by its French name 'Pisé'. Earth is extracted from the ground and compacted in layers inside specially constructed formwork. After compaction the formwork is released and moved along to a new position in the wall, or upwards to the next layer. In this way the building goes up rapidly, layer by layer, row by row.

This technique can produce buildings that are strong, durable, safe and desirable. Above all, because earth is an abundant and cheap resource, rammed earth buildings are very economical; in addition, the majority of the investment goes directly into the local economy. The method has an essential simplicity, and with its unskilled labour intensity, rammed earth can be seen as a valuable tool in the generation of low-cost housing in developing countries, in both urban and rural areas.

If well-built, rammed earth (RE) walls will compare favourably with other masonry materials, such as burnt clay bricks or concrete blocks, in compressive strength, erosion by moisture or seasonal changes of dimension. Costs will also, in most cases, be highly competitive. It must be remembered, though, that 'earth' varies in quality just as bricks or concrete blocks do. Standards of comparison are needed.

This code of practice does **not** cover blocks made of earth. To achieve comparable standards using earth blocks, a greater degree of production and site control is needed than with RE.

Mature topsoil, useful for growing plans, **must not** be used: throughout this guide **soil** means **subsoil**, and **earth** also means **subsoil**.

Nowadays, the selection and testing of soils for building can be done with some precision, and there are good techniques available to stabilize or protect earth walls from water damage and shrinkage. This document aims to show that, with adequate control and protection, buildings built in rammed earth can achieve high standards. The document will set down definitive standards by which rammed earth buildings and building techniques can be judged.

The document can be used by:

- **local builders** to show the basic standards that will achieve long-lasting results;
- **larger contractors and designers** as an outline specification for rammed earth;
- **official building regulators** to show how to judge the suitability of any rammed earth structures under their control;
- **loan and aid agencies** to give assurance on durability/mortgageability.

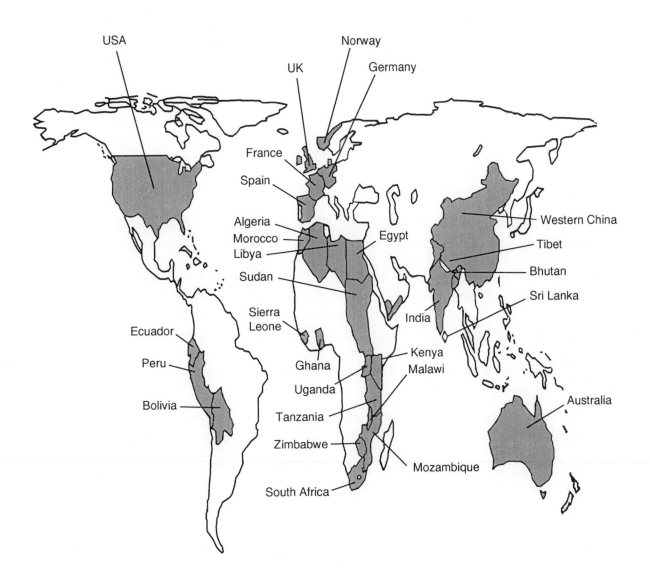

Rammed earth is found worldwide

Site selection

When choosing a building site, many factors must be considered.

o The availability of **suitable soil** is essential. Good earth for ramming must have a high sand content, some gravel, and just enough clay to act as a binder. Usually, suitable soil can be found, but if it is not nearby, moving it to the site may cost too much. Soils can be mixed to improve them: for example, a clay-rich soil can be mixed with a clay-lean one to give the correct proportions (see Part A). The soil needed may lie underneath an alluvial or sand cover, so it is essential to dig down.

o What materials and skills are available to make **formwork**? If more sophisticated forms are wanted, can they be made or must they be imported? Good formwork can be re-used many times, and can be easily repaired (see Part B).

o What other **building skills** are available? Rammed earth needs fewer skilled masons than other types of masonry building. Unskilled people are usually plentiful, and most of the work can be done by them.

o What **rainfall** may be expected? The guide maps three main zones in Africa:

less than 200mm a year   desert
200-1000mm   intermediate
more than 1000mm a year   high rainfall

High rainfall will require more protection of walls by roof overhangs and better site drainage (see Parts C and D).

o Is the site well or poorly **drained**? Poor drainage must be dealt with even if high rainfall is not expected. Stabilization of foundations may be needed in both cases (see Part C).

o What **services** are nearby? Water, electricity, roads/transport? A good water supply will be needed during building (see Part F).

o How likely is it that the building will be **maintained** when finished? A home-owner is more likely to do this than a tenant paying rent (see Part F).

o What are the local building practices? These can often give useful guides to siting, drainage, orientation and so on.

o May **earthquakes** occur? This guide maps three levels of seismic risk in Africa, based on historical records. Local fault lines may indicate local risks. If building in areas of moderate or high seismicity, it is still possible to use rammed earth, but certain extra precautions must be taken, which are described in Part G. Read this part before deciding whether RE is appropriate or not.

* If the site for building must be in a particular place, and no suitable soil is nearby, then rammed earth building will be expensive, and another method should be considered.

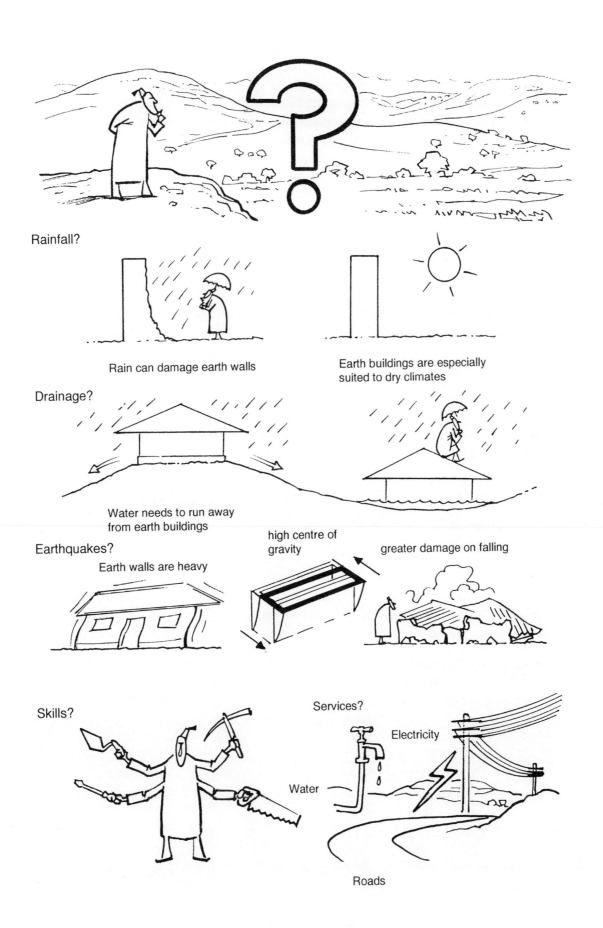

Rainfall?

Rain can damage earth walls

Earth buildings are especially suited to dry climates

Drainage?

Water needs to run away from earth buildings

Earthquakes?

Earth walls are heavy

high centre of gravity

greater damage on falling

Skills?

Services?

Electricity

Water

Roads

Site selection

Site organization

The soil is best excavated on or near the building site. Several small holes, or an overall 'scrape' is preferred to creating a large hole (unless a large hole will be used for some purpose such as a basement). Holes will attract rubbish, then vermin; they may fill with water, then breed mosquitoes. They are a health risk. (Note: if an overall scrape is planned, remember to stockpile or leave aside any soil containing organic matter for use in planting or landscaping.)

What building team will be used? This may be one person, ten people, or a hundred people. Each will need a quite different approach.

One person must do everything: dig the soil, set up the formwork, mix and place the soil, ram it, check for accuracy and quality.

Ten people will need to be organized as a team with one member acting as a supervisor, responsible for quality control and progress, but also placing the formwork with the rest of the team. The remaining people will take turns in digging the soil, placing it in the formwork, ramming the soil, and helping to move the forms.

A hundred people will need to be divided into teams, each building a defined part of the job, and separate skilled supervisors will check on quality and progress.

The equipment to be used must be chosen with care too, especially the formwork. If the soil can be used without the need for a stabilizer, and is on site, then simple equipment will be enough for moving it (barrows, headpans), but if it must be moved far then more expensive methods (dump-trucks, tipper lorries) will be needed.

If there are time limits by which the work must be finished, then a programme should be worked out against which to compare progress. In some cases the use of cement stabilization should be considered where cost and availability allow. This can speed up the work as it allows walls to be built higher within one day.

The relative size of the different teams will need to be considered so that the delivery of watered, mixed soil matches the rate of ramming, and the rate of formwork setup. This is especially true when stabilizers are used, as these must be placed before they have hardened.

Once the work is understood, it should be possible for each team of nine people to set up a medium to large form, mix, place and ram the soil twice each morning and twice each afternoon, thus completing 6 to 10m^2 in a day.

One person

Ten people

Site organization

INTRODUCTION

7

Soil classification

Soil is formed from bedrock by the action of weathering. How soils develop is a complex process, and the depth of soil over the bedrock will vary widely. However, it is usually possible to see three layers of material:

o **topsoil**, in which plants may grow, and which will contain organic matter;

o **subsoil**, with little or no organic matter in it, and which is the layer from which useful building material will come;

o **bedrock**, which will partly determine what subsoil will form.

Four main grades of material size are found, though not all may be found in any particular subsoil: gravel, sand, silt and clay.

- gravel   60.00 – 2.00mm

- sand   2.00 – 0.06mm

- silt   0.06 – 0.002mm

- clay   less than 0.002mm

Gravel and **sand** can be graded by sieving. They remain the same size whether wet or dry. So too does **silt**, but silt is more difficult to sieve, and finding out the proportion of silt to clay is difficult. Gravel, sand and silt need something to bind them when used in building.

The natural binders are colloids, of which **clay** is the most common. Clay is sticky when damp, and hard when dry; when wet it swells, and when dry it shrinks, which often results in cracking.

Clays vary, but unlike the larger grades their particles are flat and are bound to each other by a thin coating of water, even when they are 'dry'. When the surplus water in clay dries out, the particles get closer together ('shrink'); when wetted, the moisture pushes the particles apart, and the clay 'expands'. The flat plates help the other grades of soil to pack closely together when damp, but a little goes a long way.

Classification of soils may be done by referring to the main ingredients present. Thus:

Rock	**Gravel**	**Sand**	**Silt**	**Clay**
Rocky-gravel	Sandy-gravel	Sandy-silt	Silty-clay	
	Silty-gravel		Sandy-clay	
	Gravelly-silt		Clayey-sand	

Each bedrock will yield different qualities of gravel, sand, silt and clay; and, of course, the action of erosion will mix those materials in different ways. This is why study and testing are needed.

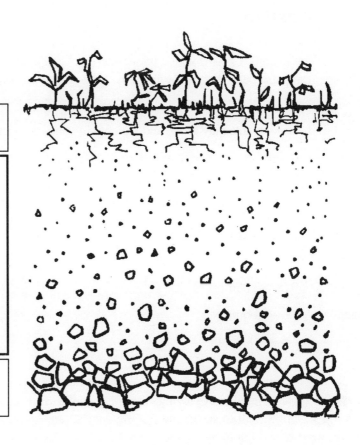

Topsoil with organic material		
Building material comes from **Subsoil** (any stray roots etc should be removed)		
Bedrock		

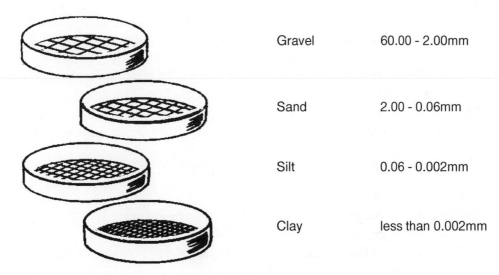

Gravel	60.00 - 2.00mm
Sand	2.00 - 0.06mm
Silt	0.06 - 0.002mm
Clay	less than 0.002mm

Soil classification

INTRODUCTION

Lateritic soils

Many African soils are classified as 'lateritic'. Many of these are red as they contain iron, which will colour a soil red at quite low concentrations; in fact, aluminium is, in most cases, the dominant metal ingredient. However, colour may range from black to yellow ochre; and red soils are not necessarily lateritic.

Soils develop from their parent rock over very long time-scales, and if left undisturbed will tend to lie in defined layers from topsoil, through ever larger particles, down to the parent rock below.

However, very different results will develop due to erosion and drainage conditions. If the water-table rises each season towards the surface, then material leached downwards will be carried back up in the form of salts, and remain there after evaporation.

Laterites develop most easily where there is a mean annual temperature of 25°C or more, where there are both warm and wet periods, where there are land slopes of moderate gradient (5° to 30°) and where groundwater fluctuates seasonally.

Because laterites **develop**, and because their characteristics change as they 'mature', care must be taken when a building project using laterite is planned. 'Immature' or young laterites may show 'self-hardening' when exposed to air, though this process is not fully understood. Another important property is the aggregation of clay-sized particles which may reduce the amount of water the clay can absorb. Also the actual clay content of the soil may be masked, since the aggregated particles appear as sand or gravel. Some soils are irreversibly changed when dried, to the point of resisting water penetration; water may also be driven off where soil is oven dried at 105°C, and give a false impression of moisture content.

Many of these qualities in laterites make for useful building performance, but also for laboratory test-results that do not reflect how the soil will perform in the field. This code, therefore, emphasizes the importance and relevance of field tests which follow as closely as possible the methods that will be used in the building work itself, and on testing the actual compressive strength of the sample or wall.

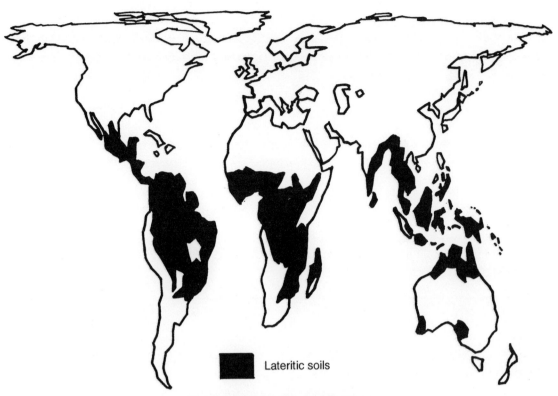

Worldwide laterite distribution

Lateritic soils

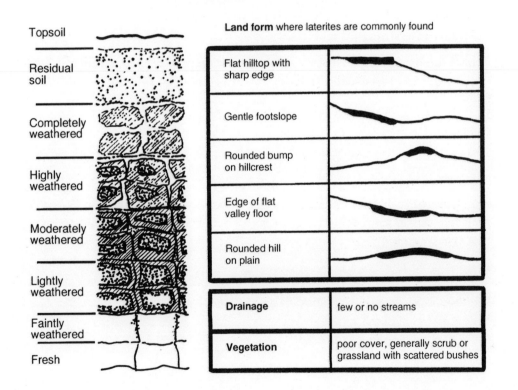

Topsoil

Residual soil

Completely weathered

Highly weathered

Moderately weathered

Lightly weathered

Faintly weathered

Fresh

Land form where laterites are commonly found

Flat hilltop with sharp edge	
Gentle footslope	
Rounded bump on hillcrest	
Edge of flat valley floor	
Rounded hill on plain	

| **Drainage** | few or no streams |
| **Vegetation** | poor cover, generally scrub or grassland with scattered bushes |

Soil analysis

The use of a suitable soil is fundamental to successful rammed earth (RE) building. Ideally, the soil should have a high sand/gravel content, with just enough clay to act as a binder and assist soil compaction. The following simple tests will help to identify soil types and may identify soils which are unsuitable for building:

o **Observation:** cracking in dry soil suggests a high clay content, while a dry soil which is loose and grainy suggests sand. Take a damp lump of soil and cut it in half with a blade: the cut surface of a plastic clay soil will be smooth and bright, whilst a silty or sandy clay will have an opaque surface, possibly crumbly when there is a large amount of sand in the soil.

o **Touch:** rub the soil between the fingers and you will be able to tell if the particle size is coarse or fine. Clay soils feel smooth and, when damp, stick; when dry, powdery. Silt will feel fairly smooth, but not sticky. Sand will feel gritty.

o **Smell**: this can identify the presence of organic matter, which has a musty smell, especially when the soil is damp and warm.

o **Local enquiry** can be very helpful. For instance, road-builders may already know of good sources of soil.

Having located by these means a potentially suitable soil, there are three ways of learning more about that soil:

o **carry out a range of field tests on soil samples, to know what the soil is made of;**

o **use the soil on site to make a small rammed earth sample – then test this sample using the 'compressive strength' field tester;**

o **carry out a range of laboratory tests (including those needed to find out the sensitivity of the soil to the test procedures) to know more exactly what the soil is made of.**

The decision as to which of these three to follow will depend on the scale of building work proposed, and the availability of test equipment. The quickest and simplest will be the second, provided there is a field tester for use. Then this on-site test can be done:

> Prepare a rammed earth test cube, then use the non-destructive tester on this cube not less than eight hours later. If this cube shows a compressive strength of 0.5 to 0.75N/mm² it can be expected to increase in strength over a week by two or three times, and thus pass the requirement for single-storey buildings.

Whether or not the first or second test route is followed, a large or important project should also include full laboratory tests, to permit a more detailed specification. Soil samples will be needed.

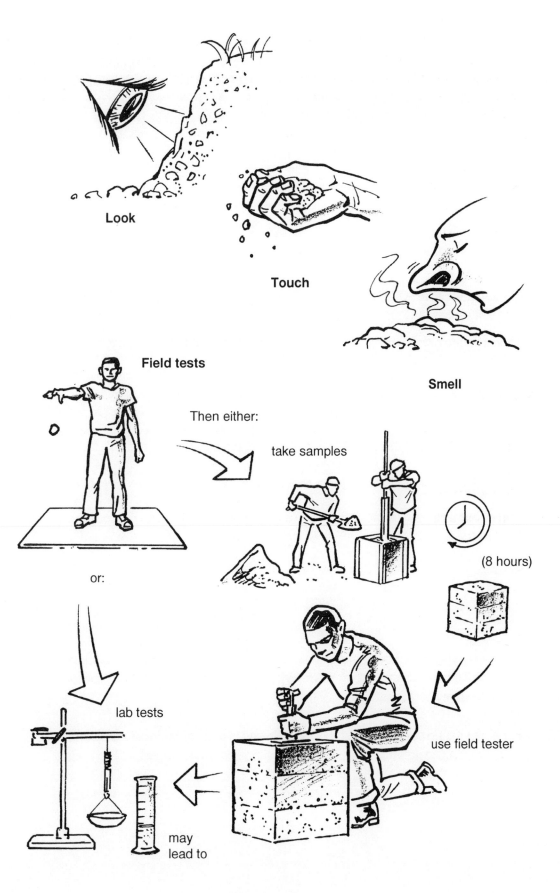

Look

Touch

Smell

Field tests

Then either:

take samples

(8 hours)

or:

use field tester

lab tests

may
lead to

Soil analysis

The soil for tests, whether in the field or for more exact laboratory tests, should be taken from the subsoil. In every case the depth should be recorded. Samples close to the surface may be useful as there may be a high yield of 'nodules' in lateritic soils (these may be sieved out for use in building), and the depth of any soil having high organic content should also be recorded. Soils vary over short distances, and therefore several samples should be taken from the area where you expect to get soil for building. Because each soil profile may contain several soil types, note and test each layer. Each sample for testing should weigh about 20kg for detailed testing as described in Part A, or for more detailed laboratory tests.

This code is intended to be suitable for all rammed earth building. However, to the extent that it is applied to affordable and low-cost projects, it is important to avoid over-specifying as this will have a direct effect on cost. The **required** tests must be done to ensure safety and durability, but the **optional** tests may in some cases represent an increase in standards beyond what is needed to produce a plain, safe and mortgageable result.

How to use the code

The document is divided into parts relating to the different stages of the building process. Each part sets out a guide relating the aims and means to achieve those aims. This leads to a definitive **standard** that will determine the minimum necessary to achieve strong, durable and sound buildings. In most cases there will be a simple test procedure to establish this standard and in some cases 'deemed to satisfy' provisions are given. Tests are numbered as 'N' to indicate that the test is **needed** for the code (there are five of these), or 'O' to show it is **optional** (there are eleven). The 'N' tests are essential, and at least one of each **must** be carried out where the code is being applied.

It is intended that the diagrams and drawings should be read with the guidance and standards for ease and clarity.

Taking samples

INTRODUCTION

15

Part A: Materials

A1 SOIL

Guide

Good **soil selection** is essential to achieving high standards in rammed earth, particularly in non-stabilized earth. There are three ways of making a choice:

- ○ carry out a range of field tests on soil samples to know what the soil is made of;

- ○ use the soil on site to make a small rammed earth sample – then test this sample using the 'compressive strength' field tester, or the 'test cube' procedure (alternative tests N/4);

- ○ carry out a range of laboratory tests (including those needed to find out the sensitivity of the soil to the test procedures) to know more exactly what the soil is made of.

Soil for rammed-earth wall-building should have a high sand content with just enough clay in it to act as a binder, and to assist in soil compaction. Too much clay will prevent good compaction, however, and can give shrinkage problems. A good range of particle sizes is the ideal.

Whichever method of selection is being used, the testing that goes with this should be done regularly. If possible, it is recommended to know the particle size gradation and plastic limits of the soil. These tests can be done in a laboratory or following the description later in Part A.

Lateritic soils are often particularly good for rammed earth, but they vary in the mix of particles as much as any other soil, and must be studied with equal care. Laterite is formed from weathering of certain rocks and is found over large areas in the tropics. Road-builders tend to use lateritic soil where possible, and may help to find sources of laterite. However, care must be taken to avoid testing by methods that will change this soil in ways that would not be the case on a real building site.

Where soil is taken from a pit in order to achieve a mix of particle size (for example, silt from upper layers and aggregate/nodules lower down) digging from a 'cliff' of material may ensure the start of a good mix.

Winning soil from a hillside may pose special problems and opportunities, and a 'scrape' may give not only a flat terrace suitable for building on, but also a mix of particle size if the strata follow the slope.

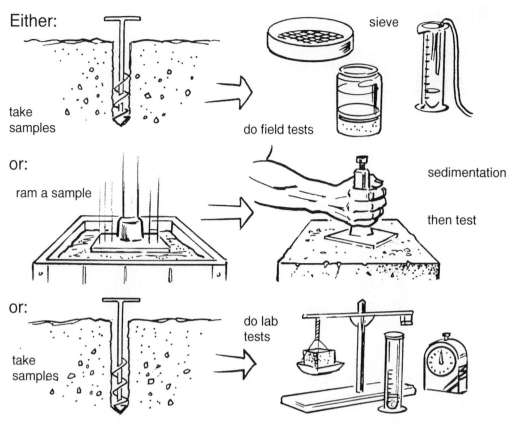

Either:

take samples

do field tests

sieve

or:

ram a sample

sedimentation

then test

or:

take samples

do lab tests

Taking samples

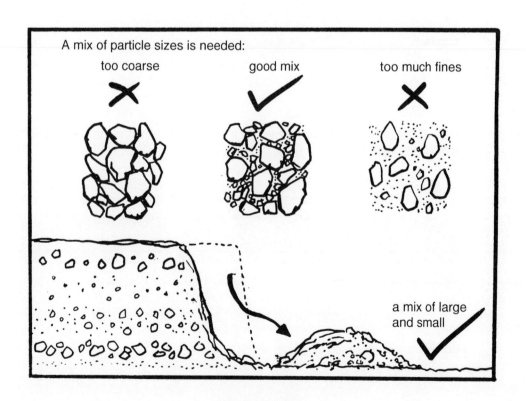

A mix of particle sizes is needed:

too coarse ✗

good mix ✓

too much fines ✗

a mix of large and small ✓

Soil selection

A1: SOIL

17

FIELD TEST N/1 : 'ROLL' TEST

Purpose

To find if soil is suitable for rammed earth.

Step one:

Take a handful of unsieved soil, moisten, make into a ball, and leave to dry in the sun. If it falls apart it has too little clay, and is thus unsuitable for rammed earth: look for another soil source.

Step two:

If the ball remains together when dry, crush the soil to remove any lumps. Add water slowly. Make a ball and place it on hard ground. Take a 10mm diameter reinforcing bar, 500mm long, and stand it vertically, with its end resting on the middle of the ball of damp soil. Let it sink in under its own weight. (Do **not** push it.) When the bar sinks in exactly 20mm the water content is right for doing the test.

Step three:

Take enough of the damp soil to form a ball in your hands; then between your hands form into a roll 25mm thick and 200mm long. Place the roll on a table, and push it gently over the edge. Measure how long it gets before it breaks off. Check the length of the piece that drops.

Result:

If the roll breaks off less than 80mm, there is not enough clay. If the roll breaks off longer than 120mm, there is too much clay.

Note: all other tests in this section are optional, but depending on resources available, and the size and quality of the project, a reliable knowledge of the clay content and the gradation of particle sizes will be very helpful.

TEST O/1 : 'SOAP' TEST

Purpose

To find out if the soil is mainly clay or silt.

Step one:

Take a handful of the soil you are testing, and damp it slightly in a bowl. Take a lump of this soil and rub it between your hands as if washing them with soap.

PART A: MATERIALS

The 'roll' test

Ensure the soil
is damp

Dry in sun

① Make a ball

② 10mm reinforcing rod
500mm
20mm

Poor soil   Good soil

③ Form into a roll 200mm long

④ 200mm   25mm
80- 120mm

The 'soap' test

① Dampen soil

② Rub between hands

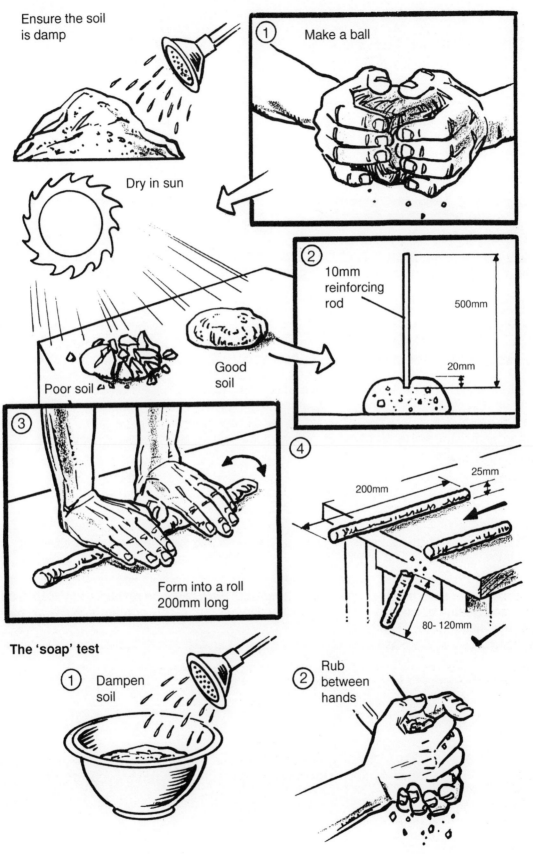

A1: SOIL

Result:

- If the soil sticks to your hands and washes off only with difficulty, the soil contains too much clay; it may need mixing with another soil before it can be used for rammed earth.
- If the soil does not stick much and washes off easily, the soil is sandy or silty; it may be usable for rammed earth as it is.

FIELD TEST O/2 : 'PARTICLE SIZE BY SEDIMENTATION'

Purpose

To find the proportions of different particle sizes in the soil without using specialist equipment.

Step one:

Have ready

- a glass jar with straight sides and flat bottom, as tall and narrow as possible, and a lid or stopper
- a measuring tape or ruler
- a watch
- a pinch of table salt
- a notebook

Step two:

Mark off on the side of the jar one third of its height.

Step three:

Fill the jar with dry soil to just over the one-third mark; compact the soil slightly and remove any soil from over the mark. Then fill the jar until it is two-thirds full of water (not more, as it could spill later). Add the pinch of salt. Mix the soil, water and salt together, then seal the top, and shake the jar vigorously until the soil particles are in suspension. Now let the jar stand for one hour.

Step four:

At the end of one hour, again shake the jar vigorously, put it down, and time one minute. When one minute is up, mark the point at which the soil has settled on the side of the jar without moving it. This is (T1), the gravel and sand fraction. Keep timing, and after 30 minutes make another mark at the point the soil has settled. This is (T2), the gravel, sand and silt combined. After 24 hours, make a third mark at the point the soil has settled. This is (T3), the gravel, sand, silt and clay fraction.

Result:

The depth of clay will be (T3)–(T2)
The depth of silt will be (T2)–(T1)
The depth of sand and gravel is (T1)

Thus the clay fraction will be: (T3)–(T2)/T3 × 100 (as a percentage)
The silt fraction will be: (T2)–(T1)/T3 × 100
The sand and gravel fraction will be: (T1)/T3 × 100
(These three should add up to 100).

> **Note: this test will show the proportions of material present, though it may yield different results from those given by formal laboratory tests if clay nodules are present, as is often the case with lateritic soils.**

PART A: MATERIALS

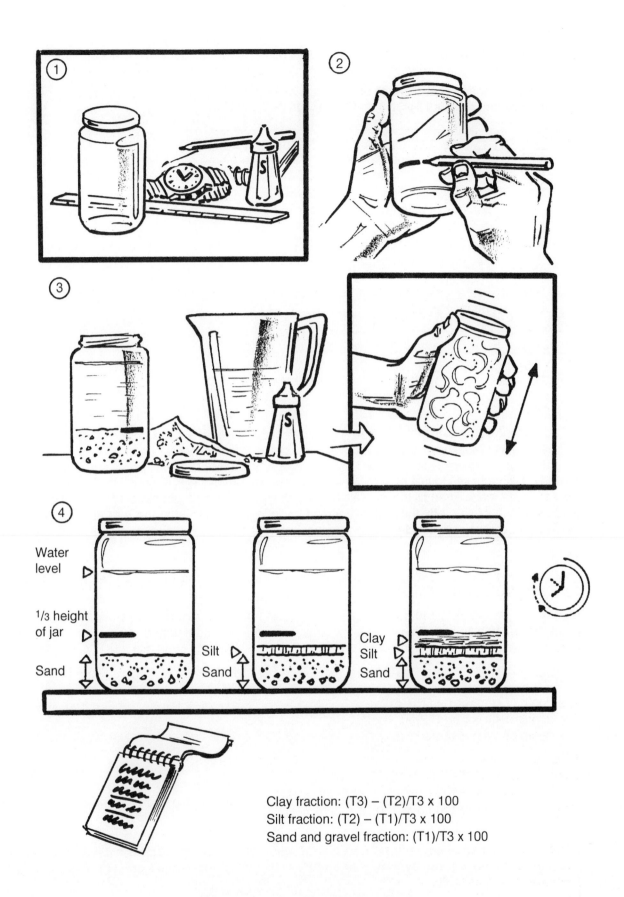

Clay fraction: (T3) – (T2)/T3 x 100
Silt fraction: (T2) – (T1)/T3 x 100
Sand and gravel fraction: (T1)/T3 x 100

'Particle size by sedimentation' test

LAB TEST O/3 : 'WET SIEVING'

Purpose

To find the larger soil particle sizes in more detail than Test O/1.

Step one:

Mix exactly 1kg sample of dry soil with water. Wash mixture through soil-testing sieves. (Use mesh sizes 6.3mm, 2.00mm, 0.425mm and 0.063mm.) Dry and weigh the portions of gravel/sand remaining in each sieve.

Step two:

Calculate the percentage of each sieve-size to the whole, and set these out in order of size. The percentage of each sieved pile to the whole pile will be: weight (in grams)/10. Thus if the pile between sieve 0.2mm and 0.02mm weighs 148g, it will be 148/10 = 14.8% of the whole.

LAB TEST O/4 : 'CLAY/SILT RATIO'

Purpose

To find the silt to clay proportion in greater detail than in Test O/1.

Step one:

Dry the silt and clay which have passed through the 0.063mm sieve. Take 100g and put into a 1-litre graduated glass measuring cylinder. Add a pinch of table salt and water up to 200mm. After twenty minutes lower a metal disc to cover material at bottom. Siphon off all water together with clay particles. Dry remaining silt and weigh it to separate proportion of silt to clay.

Step two:

Divide the result obtained in Test O/3 for the finest material into **clay** and **silt** fractions, using the step one results.

Tests relating to the plasticity of soils are shown in A4. These tests can be used to give a more detailed analysis of the soil.

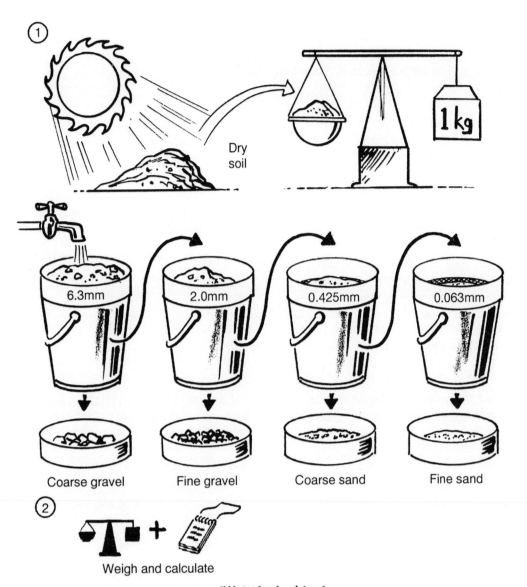

① Dry soil 1 kg

6.3mm → Coarse gravel

2.0mm → Fine gravel

0.425mm → Coarse sand

0.063mm → Fine sand

② Weigh and calculate

'Wet sieving' test

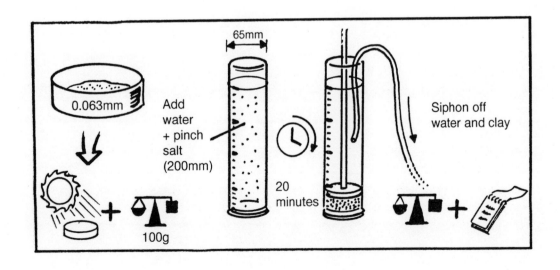

0.063mm

Add water + pinch salt (200mm)

65mm

20 minutes

Siphon off water and clay

100g

'Clay / silt ratio' test

A2 WATER

Guide

Water used for ramming should be from a clean source. However, this is less important than the *amount* of water in the soil: this will strongly affect the density which can be attained by ramming, and is called here the **Ideal Water Content (IWC)**. The IWC is important because it has a direct bearing on the strength of the finished wall. With too little water the soil cannot be properly squeezed, with too much it becomes too wet and the water itself resists compaction. The ideal amount of water will vary from one soil mix to another. Fortunately, once some experience in ramming has been gained, it becomes quickly obvious when the soil is too wet or dry.

Standard

Water used for mixing with earth for rammed earth structures shall be free of organic materials and any other harmful substances.

The mix of materials for use in rammed earth structures should have the 'Ideal Water Content', according to the 'drop' test.

FIELD TEST N/2 : 'DROP' TEST

Purpose

To find the Ideal Water Content and to check this during construction.

Step one:

Take soil that has had some water added to it. Squeeze the damp soil into a ball 40mm diameter in your hand. Then, with your arm straight out at 1.5m high (shoulder level), drop the soil ball onto a smooth clean piece of plywood (minimum 12mm thick) placed on level ground and observe the result:

- if the soil stays in one piece it is too dry: add water and try again;
- if the soil is still in one piece the clay content is too high;
- if the soil breaks into many pieces it is too wet: leave it to dry a while and try again;
- when the dropped ball breaks into only a few pieces it is close to the IWC and suitable for use.

Step two:

Continue to use the 'drop' test to check the water content of the soil as it is being used.

Note: when stabilizing with cement, slightly more water is required than shown by the 'drop' test. Do test as usual then add roughly 10% more water than test indicates.

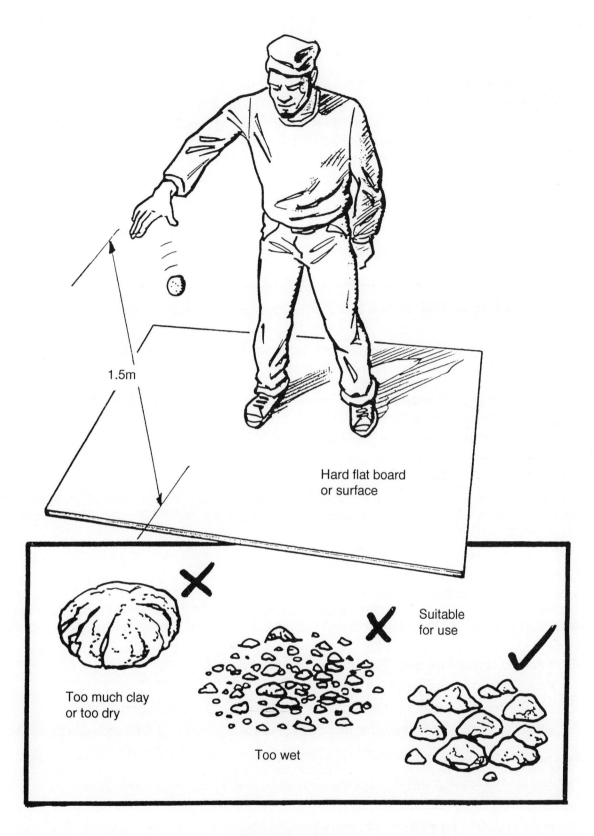

1.5m

Hard flat board
or surface

Too much clay
or too dry

Too wet

Suitable
for use

The 'drop' test

A more detailed way of finding the IWC is by testing the dry density of the material after compaction through a range of water contents:

LAB TEST O/5 : 'COMPACTION' TEST

Purpose

To find the maximum density possible by using a mould of a given volume and a constant amount of compaction, then varying the water content of soil samples until the maximum density is obtained.

Step one:

- a balance accurate to at least 0.1g (to 0.01g is better)
- a straight edge
- a mould 150 × 150 × 150mm (which gives a volume of 0.003375m³ or 3.375 litres), and with a removable upper extension to contain the loose earth whilst tamping
- a rammer with a 145mm square base and weighing 7.5kg
- a metal drying tray big enough to hold the sample and drying equipment

Step two:

Start with a very dry mix, and carry out tests increasing the moisture content by 2% each time. Mix each sample dry, adding any stabilizer, and then sprinkle water to get an even mix. Place soil in mould to a depth of 100mm when loose. Then tamp using eighteen heavy blows. Repeat twice more; the third layer will need the use of the extension piece. Then remove the extension and smooth the top surface using the straight edge and tamp. Now quickly weigh the sample after removing from the mould (W1).

Step three:

Place the soil sample on the drying dish, taking great care that no material is lost. Dry until no further weight change occurs and weigh the sample. This is the dry weight (W2). The original weight of moisture contained (M) is calculated as follows:

M = W1 − W2kg

Divide the result by 0.03375 to arrive at the percentage of water in the cube (because the sample volume was 3.375 litres).

Step four:

Keep repeating the tests, adding 2% water (0.07 litres) at each mixing, until a maximum dry weight value (W2) is found; the water content used for the cube which had the highest dry weight will be the ideal water content, given as a percentage. This makes it easy to apply the results on site if soil measuring boxes are used.

> **Note: to avoid misleading results when testing lateritic soils, it is necessary to mix gently and dry slowly.**

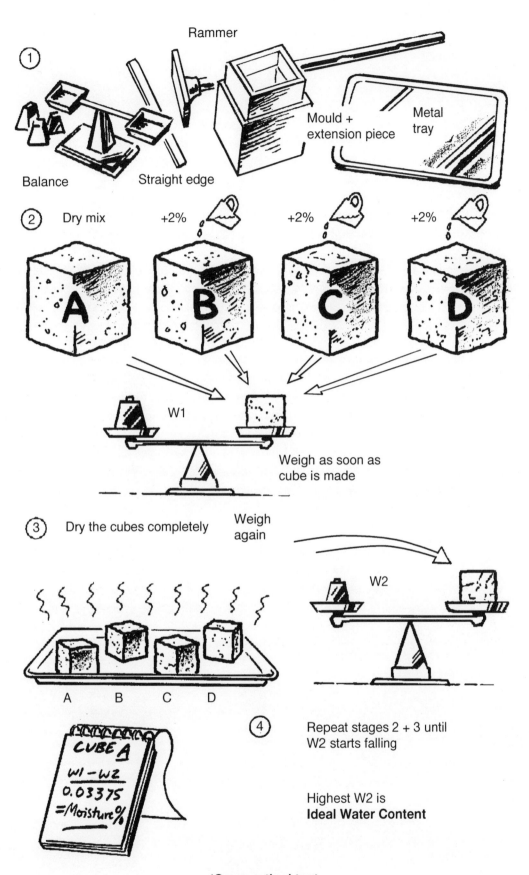

① Rammer

Balance   Straight edge   Mould + extension piece   Metal tray

② Dry mix   +2%   +2%   +2%

A   B   C   D

W1

Weigh as soon as cube is made

③ Dry the cubes completely   Weigh again

A   B   C   D

W2

④ Repeat stages 2 + 3 until W2 starts falling

Highest W2 is **Ideal Water Content**

CUBE A

W1 – W2

0.03375

= Moisture %

'Compaction' test

A3: MIXING AND BLENDING

A3 MIXING AND BLENDING

Guide

MIXING

Good mixing is important as the resultant strength of the rammed earth will depend on this. Even if only one source of soil is being used (without stabilizer), turning over the soil so that the particles are well distributed is still valuable. Mix **dry** first; if water is to be added, do this just before ramming.

Mixing must be done where the materials will not pick up other material, such as a nearby surfaced road, or a completed house base, or sheet material moved to site for this purpose. Manual mixing by turning the pile of soil with a shovel is most common. Mechanical techniques are possible, although mechanical mixing of wet mixtures presents problems. The ordinary drum concrete mixers will get soil sticking to their blades. A drum or open-ended barrel with blades fixed to a central rotating shaft is better (e.g. a pug-mill); if a front-loader is available this can be used like a huge shovel and can work well.

Before starting to mix, establish the ideal water content (IWC – see A2) which will usually be between 8% and 16%. When ready for ramming, the soil will appear quite dry. Assuming water must be added to reach the IWC, work out how many cans must be added to each wheelbarrow or batching box so that the mixing can be done consistently, either by volume or by weight. Water should be sprinkled on so that no part gets saturated; if no watering can is available, flick water on with hands from a bucket rather than pouring directly onto a flattened heap. Turn the heap while sprinkling on the water. When no cement is being used, do **not** mix by forming a 'hole' in the heap.

BLENDING

Blending is a very useful way to improve a soil which lacks a range of particle sizes. A soil which has little or no clay will need soil from another source that is 'clay-rich' so that, when blended, the grains slide over each other to form a much denser mass than before. A soil which starts out with too much clay, so that it easily cracks when drying out, will benefit from the addition of pure sand or gravel. Before deciding on the best mix, it will be useful to do a 'shrink-box' test, using the proposed blended soils.

Soil raked out before mixing with cement

Vertical mixer

Pug-mill

Rotovator

Front loader

Mixing

TEST O/6 : 'SHRINK-BOX' TEST

Make a box out of wood or metal with internal dimensions of 600 × 40 × 40mm. The box should have a bottom but no top. Oil the inside surfaces.

Note: a smaller box, say 300 × 30 × 30mm, may be used, provided very accurate measuring is done throughout: interpretation will then use shrinkage sizes half as large.

Take a sample of the soil intended for blending (or stabilization) and moisten it to its IWC (see A2). Tamp the soil firmly into the box and smooth off surface. Dry the contents for three days in the sun, or other very warm place. (Rapid drying out is important). When the sample is completely dry, push all the soil, including separated lumps, tightly up to one end of the box, and measure the shrinkage.

The results can be interpreted as follows:

Shrinkage	Interpretation
12mm or less	soil is satisfactory without cement – may need more clay
12mm–24mm	add 5% cement, or add low-clay soil (sand/aggregate)
over 24mm	too much clay for cement – consider adding low-clay soil

The 'roll' test, or other more detailed test, should be carried out where possible at regular intervals to ensure that the mix is working.

The cost of transporting the soil used for mixing/blending will have to be thought of; if only a small proportion of blend material is needed, and if this is nearby, then it is likely to be cheaper than any other alternative. However, if a large proportion of blend material is needed, or it is far from the site, then stabilization may prove more economic (see A4).

Before mixing, break up larger lumps of earth with the back of a spade.

Standard

Soils should be well mixed prior to ramming, if:

o   there is more than one source of soil to be rammed;

o   stabilizers are to be added;

o   additional water is required to achieve IWC.

Mixing by hand or by mechanical mixer should continue until there is uniform distribution of materials with uniform colour and consistency.

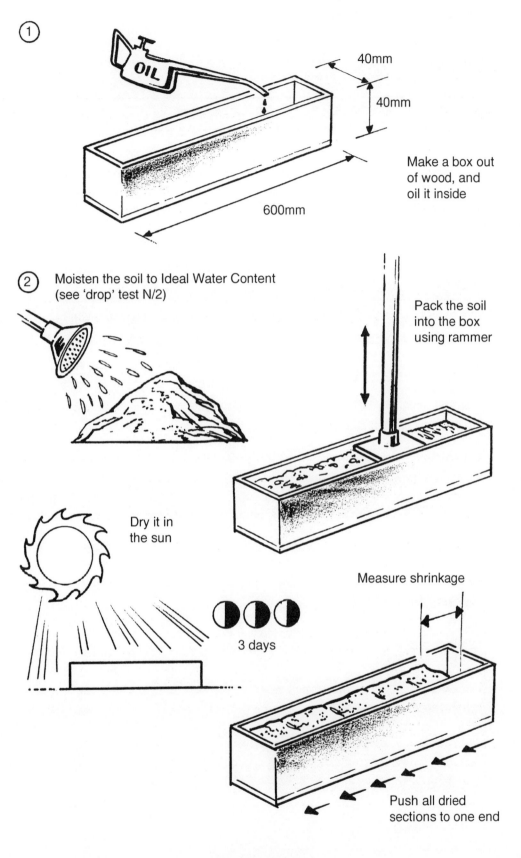

① 40mm

40mm

600mm

Make a box out
of wood, and
oil it inside

② Moisten the soil to Ideal Water Content
(see 'drop' test N/2)

Pack the soil
into the box
using rammer

Dry it in
the sun

3 days

Measure shrinkage

Push all dried
sections to one end

'Shrink-box' test

A3: MIXING AND BLENDING

A4 STABILIZATION

Guide

Various materials when mixed with soil may increase the strength of the resulting wall. This process of adding other materials to soil is called 'stabilizing'.

To stabilize or not: the arguments in favour of stabilization are:

- o speeds up building process (more useful where stabilizer cheap and/or labour expensive);
- o it improves durability and strength where the soil is poor;
- o walls may be thinner;
- o may be no need for expensive surface treatment;
- o a 'modern' building results ('soilcrete') which is distinguished from traditional materials.

The arguments against stabilization are;

- o the costs are high;
- o the materials needed may not be available, or be expensive to transport;
- o it makes the process more complicated; more things can go wrong;
- o thick walls may be desirable for climatic (or seismic protection) reasons;
- o surface treatments may be desirable for reasons of appearance.

It may be more sensible to improve the quality of the soil by importing some sand or clay-rich soil (see A3). Stabilization can be limited to those areas at greater risk: foundations and base of walls, or walls that face the prevailing wind direction. Renders may add a sufficient extra protection.

When mixing cement or lime stabilizer, it is recommended to dry the soil first. If this is impractical, a thorough mixing (repeating four or five times) will produce a satisfactory result. It is important that cement stabilized soils are rammed immediately after mixing (or at least within one hour). Once water is added, the cement will start to set.

	For		Against

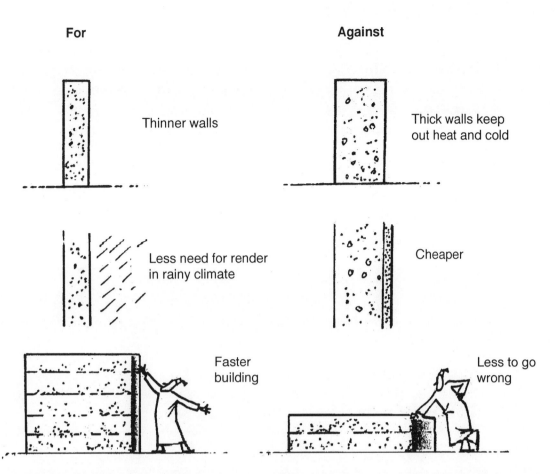

For

Thinner walls

Less need for render in rainy climate

Faster building

Against

Thick walls keep out heat and cold

Cheaper

Less to go wrong

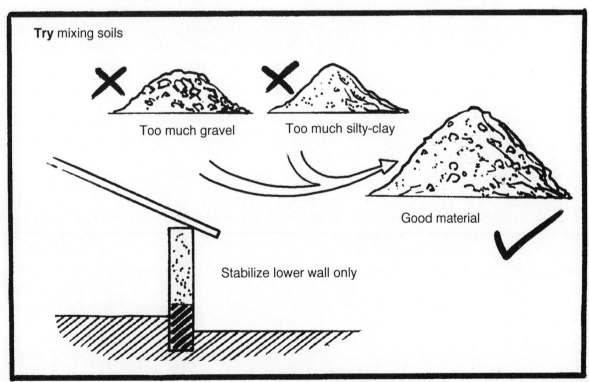

Try mixing soils

✗ Too much gravel

✗ Too much silty-clay

Good material ✓

Stabilize lower wall only

Stabilization

Specific stabilizers for rammed earth

Cement: the function of cement is to act as a binder between soil particles. The extent to which it will bind depends on the quantity of clay in the soil: it will work better on coarse sandy soils. Cement will increase compressive strength, reduce shrinkage and reduce water absorption.

Cement must be mixed well with soil, when dry, and just before ramming. Soil cement should be cured slowly, in shade, and remain damp for seven days.

Tests for strength, density, shrinkage or durability with varying amounts of cement will show the ideal mix. A guide can be determined from the 'shrink-box' test (see A3).

Lime: lime stabilizes in two ways:

- o   it modifies the clay, making the soil easier to compact;

- o   it reacts chemically with soil to form cement-like binding, but this 'pozzolanic' reaction is slow and does not work satisfactorily with all soils.

Lime can be successfully used in combination with cement for soils where neither cement on its own nor lime on its own would be successful. Either quick-lime or hydrated lime can be used. Quick lime has a drying out effect, which can be useful with very high-clay soils, but make sure there are no unslaked lumps in it. Likely dosages are between 3 and 10% by dry weight, and will increase as clay content increases. The ideal amount should be established by testing.

Pozzolanas: these are materials which contain silica or alumina. They are not cementitious themselves, but when mixed with lime or cement will then act like cement. Pozzolanas can be mixed in with lime to help speed reaction, and lower costs (if available locally). These include: fly ash, burnt clay powder, rice husk and volcanic ash. Dosage with lime or cement between 1 : 1 and 3 : 1 (pozzolana : lime/cement). Determine by testing.

Other stabilizers: there are many other traditionally used stabilizers such as whey, molasses, plant fibres and plant juices. These should be used in areas where the local tradition and expertise is already known.

Note on bitumen: since bitumen emulsion must be mixed with soil in the condition of wet mud, it is not practical for use in rammed earth walls. It is very helpful for use in surface coatings, including 'Dagga plaster', as a waterproof protection to walls in high-rainfall areas (see F2). In the USA, bitumen is called 'asphalt'.

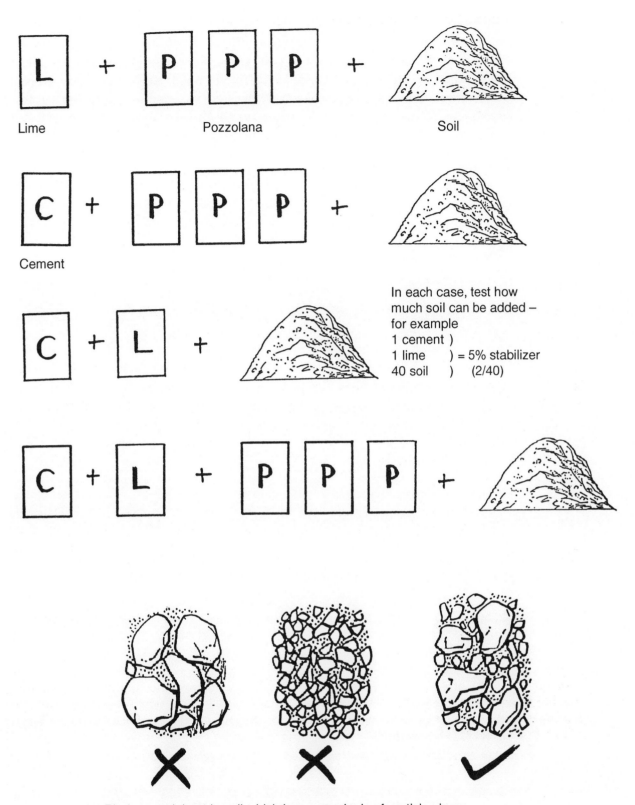

Lime   Pozzolana   Soil

Cement

In each case, test how
much soil can be added –
for example
1 cement)
1 lime   ) = 5% stabilizer
40 soil   )   (2/40)

Binders work best in soil which has a good mix of particle sizes

Stabilizer mixes

A4: STABILIZATION

Plasticity index tests

The 'Atterberg limits' tests show the respective moisture contents at which a soil changes from a liquid (viscous) to a plastic (mouldable) state, and from this state to a hard solid. This indicates the type and amount of clay present, most important in determining the choice of stabilizer; however, drying lateritic soils may give misleading results if water is 'locked' into particles. For this reason, this code calls for air-drying in every case.

The plasticity index (see Tests O/8 and O/9) can be used to indicate the appropriate stabilizer to use. (**Note:** this can be unreliable for lateritic soils). There is no substitute, however, for practical experimentation.

Test O/7 : 'LIQUID LIMIT' TEST

Purpose

To find the minimum moisture content at which soil will flow and join together.

Step one:

- a curved dish, about 10cm in diameter and 3cm deep, with a smooth or glazed inner surface;
- a grooving tool (as illustrated);
- a metal container with tightly fitting cover (e.g. large pill box);
- a balance, accurate to at least 0.1g, preferably to 0.01g.

Duration: about 10 hours.

Step two:

A sample of fine soil (about 80g) is mixed with drinkable water to a consistency of a thick paste and evenly filled into the dish such that the centre is about 8mm deep, gradually diminishing towards the edge of the dish.

This is divided into two equal parts by drawing the grooving tool straight through the middle, making a V-shaped groove (of 60° angle) and a 2mm wide gap at the bottom. Alternatively, a knife can be used.

The dish is held firmly in one hand and tapped against the heel of the other hand, which is held 30 to 40mm away. The motion must be at right angles to the groove. If it takes exactly ten taps to make the soil flow together, closing the gap over a distance of 13mm, the soil is at its liquid limit.

Step three (if needed):

If it takes fewer than ten taps, the soil is too moist; more than ten taps means that it is too dry. The moisture content must then be corrected; moist soils can then be dried by prolonged mixing or adding dry soil. The process is repeated until the liquid limit is found.

Step four:

With an accurate balance, it is sufficient to take just a small sample of soil, scraped off from a point close to where the groove closed. The sample is put into the container, which is tightly covered and weighed before the moisture can evaporate. The soil container is then placed where the soil can become completely dry. This may take more than a day, and must be checked several times, until the weight remains constant.

PART A: MATERIALS

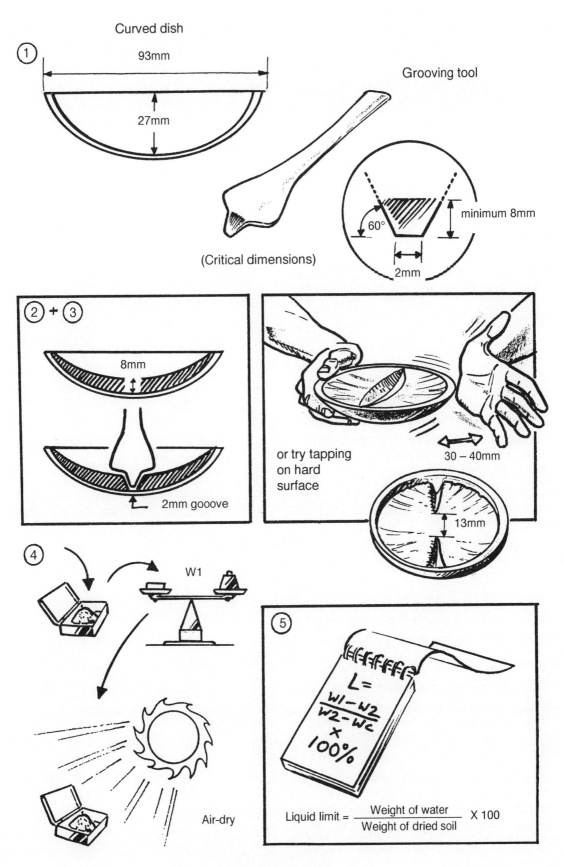

Curved dish

① 93mm

27mm

Grooving tool

(Critical dimensions)

60° 2mm minimum 8mm

② + ③

8mm

2mm gooove

or try tapping on hard surface

30 – 40mm

13mm

④ W1

Air-dry

⑤

$$L = \frac{W1 - W2}{W2 - Wc} \times 100\%$$

Liquid limit = $\dfrac{\text{Weight of water}}{\text{Weight of dried soil}}$ X 100

'Liquid limit' test

A4: STABILIZATION

Step five:

Knowing the wet (W1) and dry weight (W2) of the soil and container, and the weight of the clean dry container (Wc), the liquid limit, expressed as the percentage of water in the soil, is calculated as follows:

Liquid limit = $\dfrac{\text{weight of water}}{\text{weight of oven dried soil}}$ x 100 $L = \dfrac{W1 - W2}{W2 - Wc} \times 100\%$

Some examples of liquid limits are:
Sand: L = 0 to 30
Silt: L = 20 to 50
Clay: L = over 40

Test O/8 : 'PLASTIC LIMIT' TEST

Purpose

To find the minimum water content at which the soil is still plastic.

Step one:

- a smooth flat surface, e.g. glass plate 20 x 20cm;
- a metal container, and a balance, as for the liquid limit test.

Duration: about 10 hours.

Step two:

About 5g of fine soil (with the gravel sieved out) is mixed with water to make a workable, but not sticky, ball. This is rolled further to a length of 5cm and thickness of 6mm.

Step three:

Placed on the smooth surface, the sample is rolled into a thread of 3mm diameter (see illustration opposite for thread test). If the sample breaks before the diameter reaches 3mm, it is too dry. If the thread does not break at 3mm or less, it is too moist.

Step four:

The plastic limit is reached if the thread breaks into two pieces of 10–15mm length. When this happens, the broken pieces are quickly placed in the metal container and weighed (W1).

Step five:

The next steps of drying and weighing the soil and container are the same as for the liquid limit test, determining the values W2 and Wc.

Step six:

The whole procedure is repeated for the second half of the original sample. If the results differ by more than 5%, the tests must be repeated once again.

Step seven:

The plastic limit is calculated in the same way as the liquid limit:

Plastic limit = $\dfrac{\text{weight of water}}{\text{weight of oven-dried soil}}$ x 100 $P = \dfrac{W1 - W2}{W2 - Wc} \times 100\%$

PART A: MATERIALS

Step three

Roll until 3mm thick

If it breaks before, it is too dry;

If it does **not** break at 3mm, it is too wet

3mm gauge rod

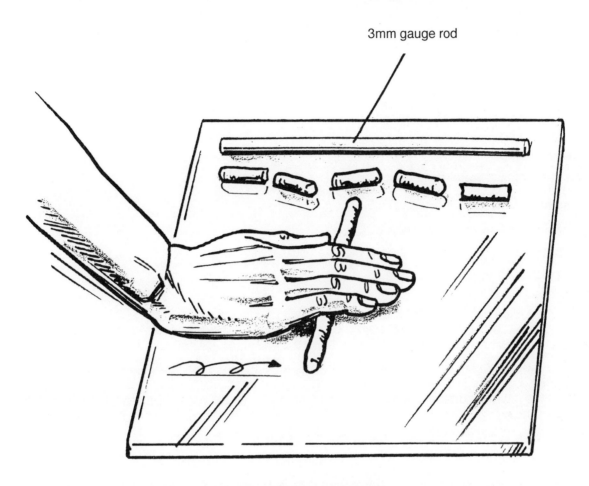

200 x 200mm glass sheet

'Plastic limit' test

Test O/9 : 'PLASTICITY INDEX'

The plasticity index (PI) is the difference between the liquid limit (L) and plastic limit (P):

PI = L – P

The simple mathematical relationship makes it possible to plot the values on a chart. The advantage is that the areas can be defined in which certain stabilizers are most effective.

It should, however, be noted that lateritic soils do not necessarily conform to this chart. There is in fact no substitute for practical experimentation, using the recommended stabilizers to begin with, and starting with small dosages.

Another valuable test to find out if enough stabilizer is being used is the 'water absorption' test. Stabilized walls should not absorb more than 15% water by weight.

Test O/10 : 'WATER ABSORPTION'

Step one:

Make three test cubes as described in D2.

Step two:

Air-dry all the cubes for 24 hours, or until significant weight-loss ceases.

Step three:

Number and weigh each sample cube, and write down their weights.

Step four:

Cover the cubes completely in unheated water (say 15°C to 25°C) for four hours; then weigh the cubes again.

Step five:

Work out how much water has been absorbed as follows:

- weight of wet cube – weight of dry cube = weight of water absorbed;
- divide the result by the weight of the dry cube, and multiply by 100 to find the percentage absorbed (take average result from three cubes).

Standard

Stabilizing materials may be added to earth for rammed earth structures – to improve strength, to improve resistance against water, or to achieve less shrinkage. Approved materials for stabilization are:

- ordinary Portland cement;
- lime or hydrated lime;
- cement or lime combined with pozzolanas;
- such other stabilizer as the building supervisor shall approve.

PART A: MATERIALS

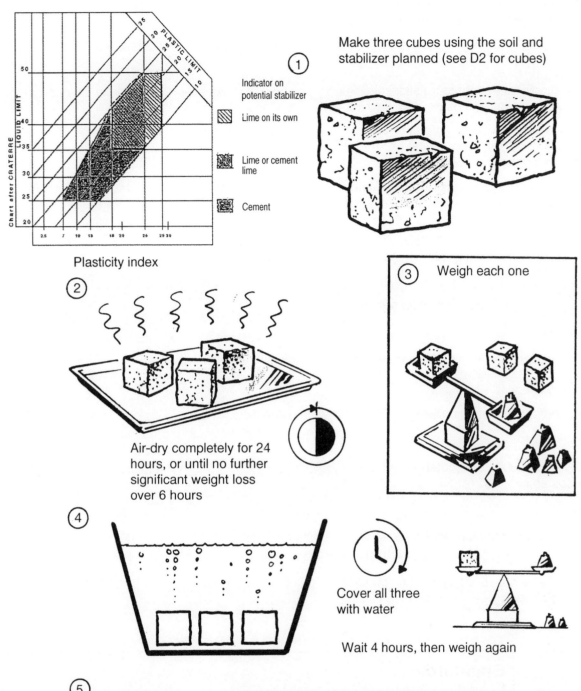

Plasticity index

Indicator on potential stabilizer

Lime on its own

Lime or cement lime

Cement

① Make three cubes using the soil and stabilizer planned (see D2 for cubes)

② Air-dry completely for 24 hours, or until no further significant weight loss over 6 hours

③ Weigh each one

④ Cover all three with water

Wait 4 hours, then weigh again

⑤

Cube	Dry Wt	Wet Wt	Water	Calc.	%
1	1.2	1.4	0.2	$\dfrac{0.2 \times 100}{1.2}$	16.7%
2	1.3	1.5	0.2	$\dfrac{0.2 \times 100}{1.3}$	15.4%
3	1.25	1.4	0.15	$\dfrac{0.15 \times 100}{1.25}$	12%

Average 16.7 + 15.4 + 12 = 44.1

$$\frac{44.1}{3} = 14.7$$

'Water absorption' test

A4: STABILIZATION

Part B: Formwork

B1 FORMWORK REQUIREMENTS

Guide

Formwork is a box without top or bottom, held together with ties. Forms may also turn corners and contain 'blockouts' to create reveals or other shapes. Forms are held vertical with stays or props. The purpose of the formwork is to contain soil while it is being rammed.

FORMWORK REQUIREMENTS

The three major components, **sides, ends** and **corners**, must each meet the following requirements to be satisfactory.

Strength and stiffness are the first all important factors, not only for the survival of the formwork but also for the correct compaction of the wall. Bulging of formwork may be prevented by using ever more ties in the box, but access must be available to the rammer so stiffness is important too.

Lightness is also a very important consideration. Lifting, assembling and aligning over-heavy cumbersome formwork will damage work in progress and may be dangerous. A guideline might be that no single item should be more than one person can lift to over head height.

Ease of alignment in all the different parts to allow fast set up and removal of the forms ensures quick work and a good finished product. Alignment includes smooth horizontal/ vertical slots, comfortable holes for bolts and smooth running bolts or ties.

Design and construction of forms will reflect the local commercial conditions and material availability. These considerations will determine the nature of the work carried out.

The modern use of stabilizing materials such as cement has changed the planning process in both stabilized and unstabilized rammed earth.

Unstabilized rammed earth is built in horizontal lengths, generally building the entire plan of a building before returning to the start to build the next higher lift.

Height for unstabilized building lift will depend on several factors:

o quality of soil: one soil will stand 2.5m high while another will only reach 0.6m at 300mm wall width;

o slenderness of the wall also determines the possible height of each lift: thicker walls may be built higher;

o self-supporting formwork allows work to continue up in some cases where heavy formwork and vibration from work in progress would damage earlier work.

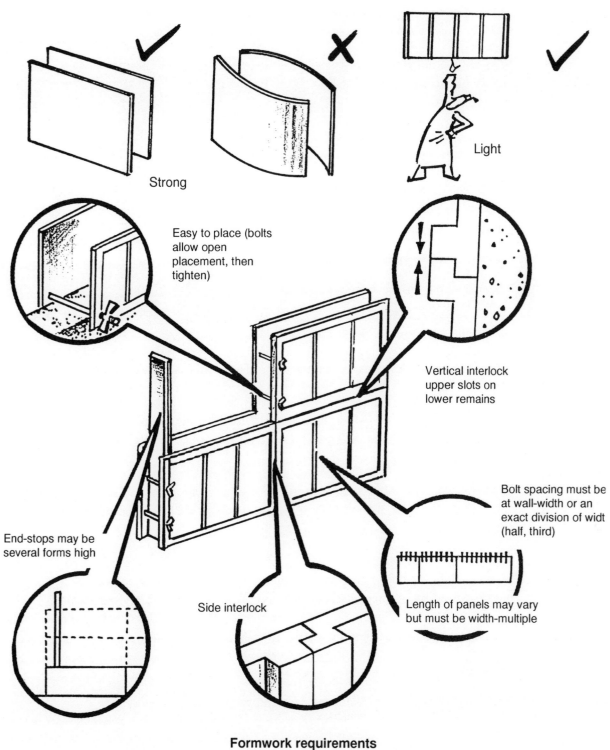

Strong

Light

Easy to place (bolts
allow open
placement, then
tighten)

Vertical interlock
upper slots on
lower remains

End-stops may be
several forms high

Side interlock

Bolt spacing must be
at wall-width or an
exact division of widt
(half, third)

Length of panels may vary
but must be width-multiple

Formwork requirements

B1: FORMWORK REQUIREMENTS

43

More sophisticated formwork will speed up work. The need for care with both horizontal and vertical joints (particularly with unstabilized work) means that the easy handling of forms is an advantage, both when setting up and when stripping down.

Whether to build with or without stabilizer involves a series of choices and may affect the quality of the end product and how it is finished, which also has implications for the formwork system chosen (see A2).

Formwork for stabilized walls (particularly cement) generally needs to be more sophisticated than for unstabilized, reflecting the cost of cement and the need to achieve a good off-form finish quickly. The basic criteria for all formwork are the same: strength, lightness and ease of alignment; but for formwork which rises vertically, the alignment is between forms rather than between formwork and wall which poses a different set of problems to the designer.

NAMING THE PARTS

The forms or sides – also called shutters

Sides may typically be made from plywood, timber planks and framing, mild steel or a combination of these.

Sides may interlock along both their vertical and horizontal edges to allow larger and higher lifts.

Sheet materials such as plywood give good off-form finished surfaces. A good quality ply will also be resistant to moisture and abrasion, though paint primer will help to preserve any timber.

Sides may also be of different heights as long as all parts are accessible with a rammer. This can be anything from 300mm high to the full height of the wall (if the thickness of wall allows a person to work inside the box comfortably).

Traditional builders often use very small forms for ease of assembly, lightness and to prevent deflection while ramming. more modern formwork is often larger as it reduces the number of assemblies, reduces handling, and relates to sheet sizes of board material and steel. A height of 600mm allows free access and doubles to 1.2m which is a commonly achievable maximum height of unstabilized wall; and many sheets are made 1.2m wide.

End stops

End stops are made from similar materials to the sides and must be as strong as the sides. Where vertical building is undertaken it helps if end stops are more than twice box height as this acts to reduce the amount of time for setting up by simply clamping additional sides to the end stops. It also gives ease of access for checking verticality of the box.

It is helpful if all corners, whether at a joint between two sections or at the corner of a building, have a chamfer to prevent them becoming ragged. This is easily achieved by fixing two long chamfer pieces to the end stops so automatically placing them at the end of each wall. This also helps to minimize the effects of shrinkage by forcing a construction joint.

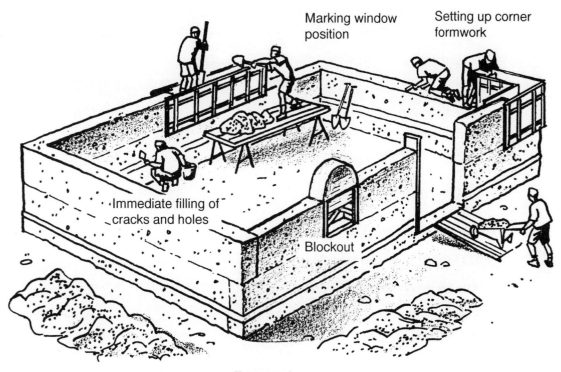

Marking window position

Setting up corner formwork

Immediate filling of cracks and holes

Blockout

Formwork

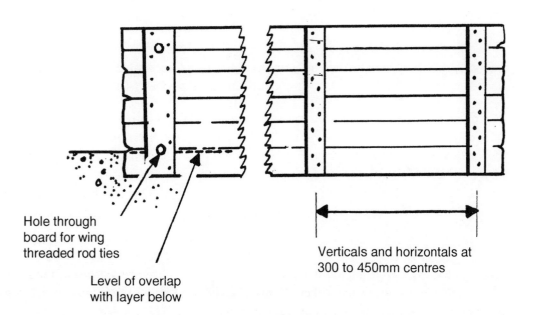

Hole through board for wing threaded rod ties

Level of overlap with layer below

Verticals and horizontals at 300 to 450mm centres

Form or sides / shutters

B1: FORMWORK REQUIREMENTS

45

Ties or bolt and spacers

The box must be held firmly together, either by direct bolting or by means of cantilever bolts. Direct through-bolting is the most common means of holding a box together, but certain points should be remembered.

A threaded tie is the most flexible and the most efficient way to through-bolt but should be smooth within the wall and only threaded at the end for ease of removal. It should have a very open thread to prevent clogging. Check on supply.

Other ties which use wedges are more difficult to use and only allow a little fine adjustment to tighten or loosen the box to an existing piece of wall. Wedge systems work best if made of metal to prevent crushing in use (which may result in variations in the wall thickness).

Many cantilever systems have been suggested, and some are in traditional use (China) but generally for work requiring a rendered finish where a rough surface may be an advantage.

Bolting formwork often requires a spacer in the box to set the width of the wall. Spacers can be sophisticated steel guides or simple lengths of timber.

Whatever the spacer is, it should be softer than the formwork to prevent damage to form faces. The main thing to remember when using spacers in the box is to remove them before they are covered up.

Corners

Building corners can be handled in two ways. The first is by bonding straight sections of wall as with bricks. This method needs little further explanation. But note: newer, thinner walls may be deflected when acting as an end stop. To prevent damage from this, the wall will need to be propped.

The other way to build corners is to have formwork which is made up or can be made up into corner sections. This method is much sounder, and will be required in earthquake areas.

Cost is a factor, but having chosen materials for the sides of the box, the corners should be a logical extension of the sides.

For some materials it may be simplest to build a large corner assembly which may be moved from corner to corner. With other systems, a corner unit acts in just the same way as a horizontal extension between two standard pieces of formwork but turning a corner; this allows building 'T's as well as 'L's.

In earthquake zones chamfers on the insides of corners are helpful in increasing stiffness at the weak point; slide the forms away from the corner on the inside face, and fit in an angled piece of the required width (see Part G).

Props or stays

Stays to ensure the verticality of the box are very important. Always prop in two directions, at right angles.

Stays

Wedge tiles (little adjustment possible)

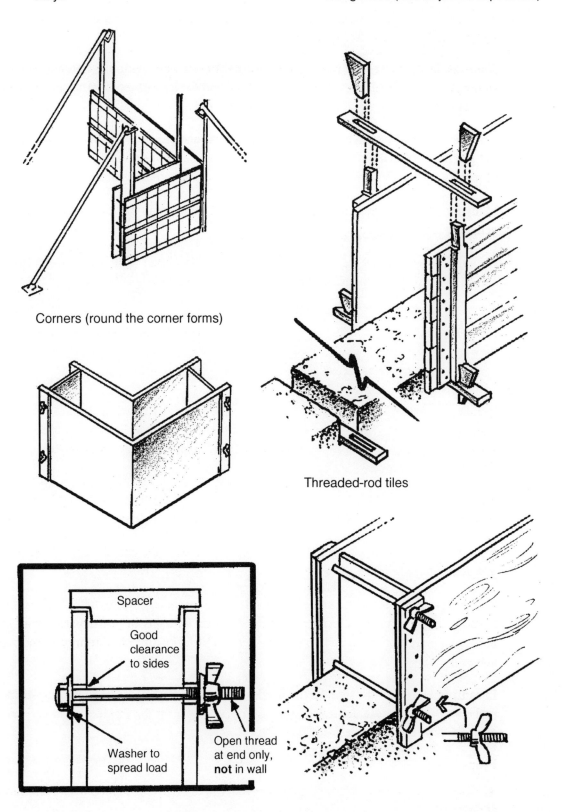

Corners (round the corner forms)

Threaded-rod tiles

Spacer

Good
clearance
to sides

Washer to
spread load

Open thread
at end only,
not in wall

Naming the parts

B1: FORMWORK REQUIREMENTS

47

Stays or props can be extremely simple 'bush' poles or state-of-the-art 'Acrow' props, lightweight and adjustable, but either way a means of quickly fixing, setting and taking apart is an advantage.

Blockouts

Full wall depth blockouts are simple to make and can speed up building of reveals and keep down costs in the long run by reducing the need for lintels and other inserts. Blockouts for arches will avoid the need for lintels altogether.

Care needs to be taken to ensure that these are both strong enough for the job and that they may be removed afterwards.

Wedges

Finally, wedges are extremely useful building tools for a variety of jobs. Wedges to chock up a box assembly before building, to adjust end stops to a vertical position, to knock out bolts with. Simple timber wedges can allow both extremely fine adjustment to a set-up or be a blunt instrument.

Standard

Formwork must allow access to all parts within formwork for compaction.

Formwork shall permit building of required wall width.

Deformation of formwork: main elements (sides, end stops and corners) shall not exceed 3mm from true position when tested by applying a 150kg load at mid-span between ties or supports.

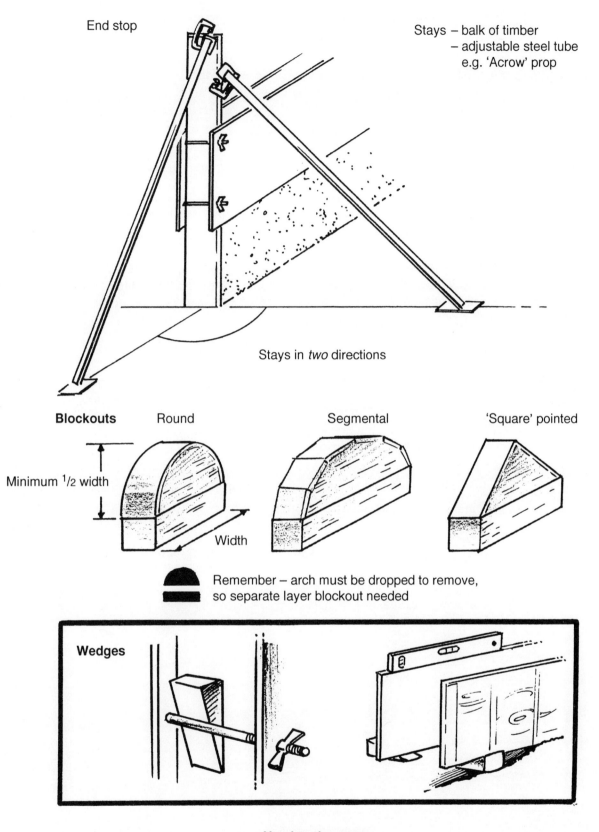

End stop

Stays – balk of timber
– adjustable steel tube
e.g. 'Acrow' prop

Stays in *two* directions

Blockouts   Round   Segmental   'Square' pointed

Minimum ¹/₂ width

Width

Remember – arch must be dropped to remove,
so separate layer blockout needed

Wedges

Naming the parts

Test N/3 : 'FORMWORK DEFORMATION'

Purpose

To find how much the formwork to be used will bend when loaded.

Step one:

Place formwork member to be tested flat, between supports (such as 50 x 50mm battens), set at the distance between ties. Place a block on each side of the mid-span, and make a mark on each showing where the formwork face is.

Step two:

Place 150kg weight (such as three bags of cement) at mid-span. Make a second mark on the two blocks to show where the formwork face now is.

Step three:

Measure the difference between the two marks on each of the two blocks; the average will be the deformation. If this is more than 3mm then either the tie spacing must be made smaller, or the formwork made stronger.

Deemed to satisfy *(frame spacing is to be both horizontal and vertical):*

Sides	15mm pine play on 14/16 gauge mild steel frame at 300mm spacing
	or
	15mm pine play on 75mm x 50mm first quality pine framing at 450mm spacing
	or
	20mm seasoned pine planks screwed to steel or timber framing as above.
End stops	15mm pine ply blocked up to 45mm depth with supports at 300mm spacing
	or
	20mm pine planking with 75 x 50mm pine framing behind at 450mm spacing.
Bolts as ties	13mm mild steel bar
	Nuts and washers to match bar thread
Corners	Where corners are an extension of form sides and not a complete unit: 14 gauge facings on 8 gauge mild steel framing, spaced as for sides. Where corners are complete unit, deformation must not exceed the standard for sides: same materials as sides.

PART B: FORMWORK

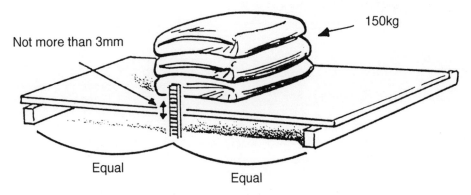

Not more than 3mm

150kg

Equal   Equal

Length between supports to be same as bolt spacing

'Formwork deformation' test

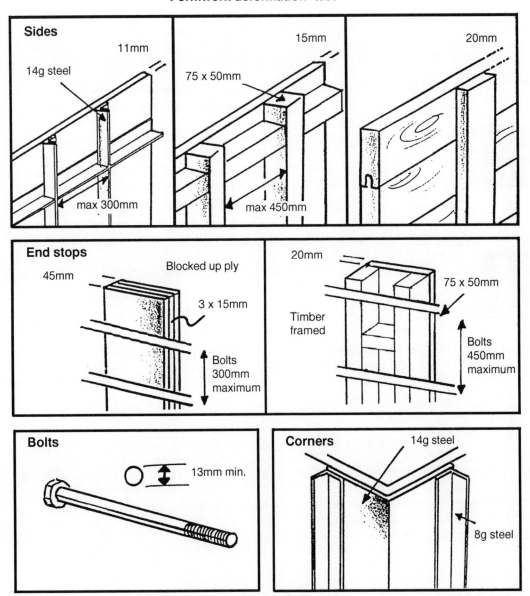

Sides

11mm

14g steel

max 300mm

15mm

75 x 50mm

max 450mm

20mm

End stops

Blocked up ply

45mm

3 x 15mm

Bolts 300mm maximum

20mm

75 x 50mm

Timber framed

Bolts 450mm maximum

Bolts

13mm min.

Corners

14g steel

8g steel

Formwork elements

B2 FORMWORK IN USE

Guide

RAMMERS (TAMPS)

Rammers or tamps can be manual or pneumatic.

Manual rammers have a handle and a head. The handle is usually between 1.5m and 1.8m long. It may be of wood or metal. If metal tube is used, the weight of the rammer can be adjusted by partly filling the handle with sand. The head can also be of metal or wood. The whole rammer should weigh between 5 and 10kg. The rammer should be dropped 150-300mm with moderate force, which will depend on the ratio of rammer weight to face area. The head should be small (80-120mm) with either a flat face and chamfered edges, or a gentle wedge shape angled at 30° to the horizontal. Differently-shaped heads are possible and should be considered after making experiments.

Pneumatic tamps are made by several manufacturers, usually driven by compressed air. The tamp face is typically circular and should be small (70-150mm). Although they will reduce the workforce, they may not produce any increase in the strength of the wall.

RAMMING

The soil should be built up in layers within the formwork, maximum 100mm thick, before ramming and compacting to 50-70mm. Where larger stones are found in the soil, care must be taken to prevent these from rolling to the formwork face by using a shovel to push ('paddle') the stones away from the sides.

Ramming should be systematically carried out, ramming along the sides first, constantly crossing from side to side to obtain an even result, then ramming the centre until the entire layer is dense and hard, producing a ringing sound when struck with the rammer. This reduces pressure on the formwork. At this stage no further impressions result from the blows. The next 100mm layer is shovelled in, and the process continues.

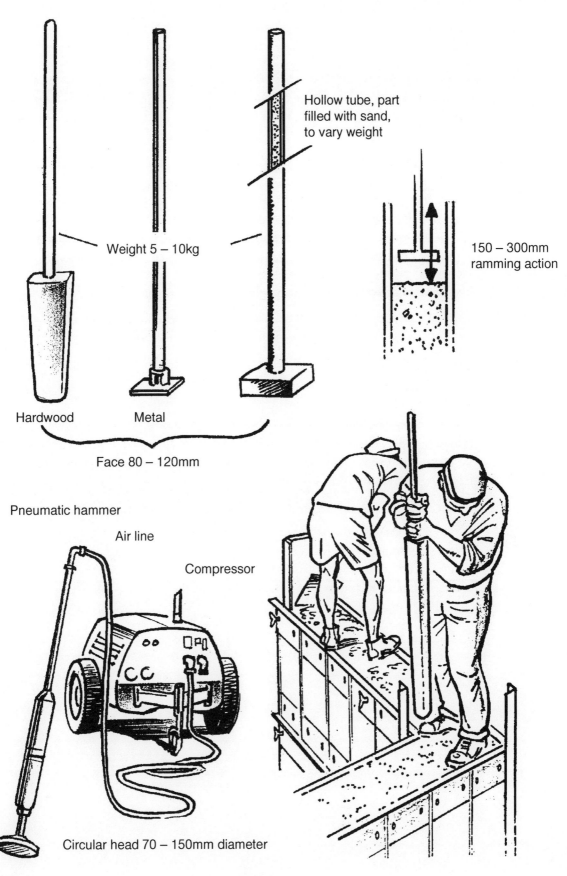

Hollow tube, part filled with sand, to vary weight

Weight 5 – 10kg

150 – 300mm ramming action

Hardwood   Metal

Face 80 – 120mm

Pneumatic hammer

Air line

Compressor

Circular head 70 – 150mm diameter

Ramming

B2: FORMWORK IN USE

SETTING UP, USING, STRIPPING DOWN

Forms should be designed with reasonable tolerances between sides and ties to prevent them from jamming. Care should be taken not to set up so that ties are awkward to remove.

Minor shifts in formwork when building can make stripping down extremely difficult and damage fresh work. To prevent formwork deformation while building, ramming should start at each fill along the edges of the box, only moving to the middle of the box when the sides are compact.

Care should be taken not to deform ties (bolts), and not to strike ties while ramming. The soil must be compacted underneath the tie, and angled blows will be needed for this.

After ties are removed, forms should be 'broken' from wall sides by 'slicing' with an upwards or sideways movement across wall faces rather than 'folding' away from the face to prevent fresh work from being damaged by sticking to the form sides.

GROUNDWORKS

Where trench foundations are to be cast, plan how to set up the formwork in the trench, and how the ties (bolts) are to be removed. Either the trench must be widened on the side for withdrawing the ties, or the forms must be wedged within the trench by some other method.

Trenches should be widened towards the centre of the building to reduce labour.

Standard

Soil shall be placed within the formwork and then rammed until it is fully compacted, so as to meet the requirements of the Test N/4 : 'Compressive strength' (see D1) or 'Test cube' (see D2).

Care must be taken when removing the formwork not to damage the work.

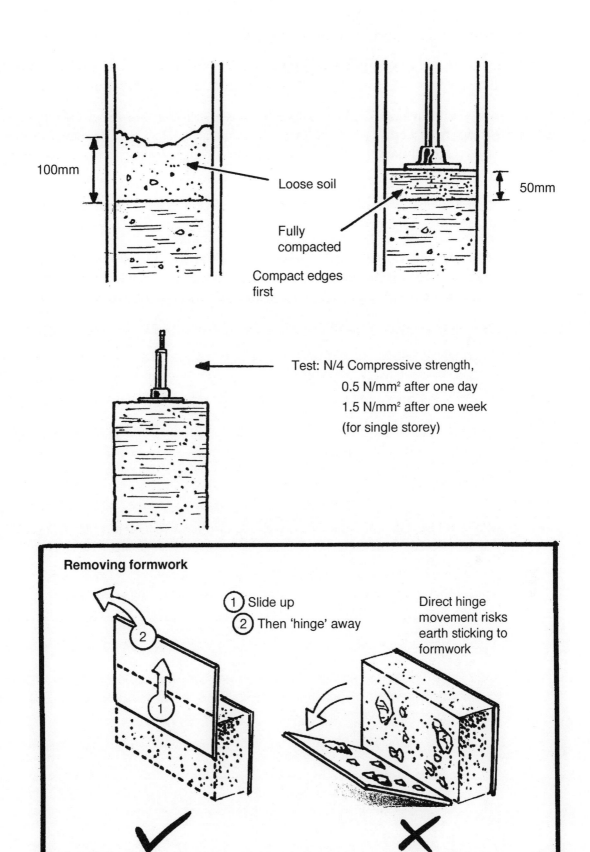

100mm

Loose soil

Fully
compacted

Compact edges
first

50mm

Test: N/4 Compressive strength,
0.5 N/mm² after one day
1.5 N/mm² after one week
(for single storey)

Removing formwork

① Slide up
② Then 'hinge' away

Direct hinge
movement risks
earth sticking to
formwork

✔

✗

Part C: Groundworks

C1 FOUNDATIONS

Guide

Always try to find a site where the subsoil is form – rock, gravel or firm sand (types I and II in Table C1). If a site has poor drainage or is liable to bogginess, flooding or seasonal cracking, stabilized foundations should be used; unstabilized earth foundations if used must be well protected since they may otherwise not remain compact – take special care.

Sites on which suitable building soil is found are generally suitable to build on.

Some soils may appear hard in dry conditions but become boggy in wet weather – for example, 'black cotton' soil. Take local advice. Dig down to firm subsoil if possible and provide a deep footing of aggregate which will also act as a 'french drain', or re-site.

Earth foundations should be used with caution; ideally an impervious coating should be placed on both sides of the foundations below ground level. Time should be allowed (several days) before backfilling. On poor sites stabilized foundations are recommended.

The ground immediately around the base of the walls should be well drained. For example, with a 'french drain' (a trench with at least 200mm deep pea-sized gravel – see illustration in C2). The drain should run to a convenient ditch, or at least well away from the building.

The surface of the ground around the base of walls can be protected from water by the use of hard paving such as rubble with filled joints. This is especially useful where the ground will swell or shrink in wet or dry seasons, such as happens in 'black cotton' soils.

Stabilization mixtures will need to be generally stronger than with walls, by 50% or more.

Care should be taken to check if there are any sulphates in the soil which may react with cement. Sulphate resisting cement may be difficult or expensive, so alternative stabilization may be better.

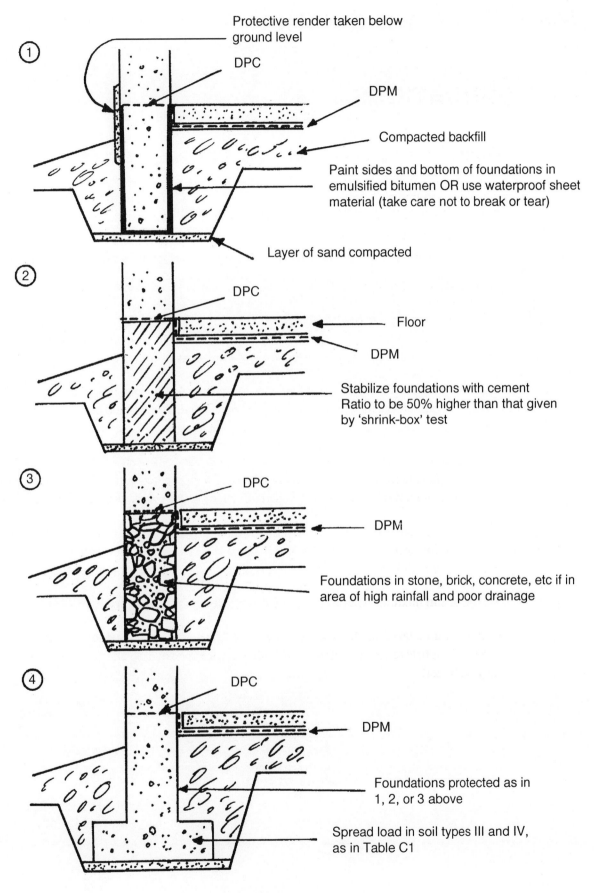

① Protective render taken below ground level

DPC

DPM

Compacted backfill

Paint sides and bottom of foundations in emulsified bitumen OR use waterproof sheet material (take care not to break or tear)

Layer of sand compacted

② DPC

Floor

DPM

Stabilize foundations with cement Ratio to be 50% higher than that given by 'shrink-box' test

③ DPC

DPM

Foundations in stone, brick, concrete, etc if in area of high rainfall and poor drainage

④ DPC

DPM

Foundations protected as in 1, 2, or 3 above

Spread load in soil types III and IV, as in Table C1

Foundations

C1: FOUNDATIONS

Table C1 Minimum width of strip foundations in rammed earth

Type of subsoil	Condition of subsoil	Field test applicable	Foundation width	Foundation thickness
I rock	not inferior to sandstone, lime-stone or firm chalk	requires at least mech-operated pick for excavation	equal to width of wall	not applicable (N/A)
II gravel sand	compact compact	requires pick for exca-vation. Wooden peg 50mm square hard to drive beyond 150mm	equal to width of wall	N/A
III clay sandy clay	stiff stiff	cannot be moulded with the fingers and requires a pick or mechanically operated spade for the removal	400mm	$\dfrac{F - W}{2}$ (minimum = wall width)
IV clay sandy clay	firm firm	can be moulded by firm pressure with the fin-gers and can be exca-vated with spade	500mm	$\dfrac{F - W}{2}$ (minimum = wall width)
V sand silty sand clayey sand	loose loose loose	can be excavated with a spade. Wooden peg 50mm square can be easily driven	750mm (so better to dig deeper firmer subsoil then apply width needed for that soil type)	
VI silt clay (and sandy/silty clays)	soft soft	fairly easily moulded in the fingers and readily excavated	800mm (so dig deeper)	
VII silt clay (and sandy/silty clays)	very soft very soft	natural sample in winter conditions exudes bet-ween fingers when squeezed in fist	1000mm (so dig deeper)	

where F = foundation width
W = wall width

PART C: GROUNDWORKS

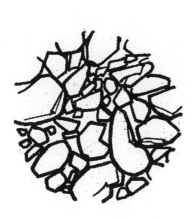

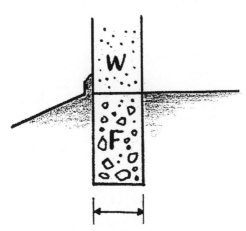

Good subsoil (rock or gravel)

Foundation width same as
wall above (minimum 200mm)

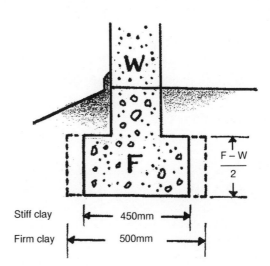

Poor subsoil

Stiff clay	450mm	
Firm clay	500mm	

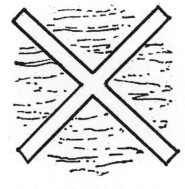

Soft or very soft clay of silts

– dig deeper to better subsoil

or

– find new site

Soft subsoil

Foundations

C2 RISING DAMP PROTECTION FOR WALLS

Guide

Damp-proof courses (DPCs) should be at least 150mm above the surrounding ground level. Increase this to 300mm in areas of high rainfall.

It is important to join any damp-proof membrane (DPM) in the floor to the damp-proof course in the wall, either by lapping (sheet materials) or sealing (liquids).

As the rammed earth wall dries out, a certain amount of shrinkage is bound to take place; the extent depending on the clay content and the speed of drying – the slower the better. Thus DPCs that remain flexible are preferable. Some DPC materials could be damaged by ramming and will need protection (for example, plastic sheet must not have coarse gravel rammed directly onto it).

Suitable materials for providing a DPC are:

Waterproof liquids	**Waterproof sheet materials**
three coats bitumen solution	thick plastic sheet
three coats bitumen/rubber emulsion	lead/aluminium/copper cored bitumen
three coats tar/rubber emulsion	
applied soft bitumen	

proprietary products approved by building surveyor

Another way to provide the DPC is to mix a concrete slurry using a water repellant, and place this in the formwork just before starting to ram the wall.

The ground immediately around the base of the walls should be well drained, using a 'french drain' (a trench with at least 200mm deep pea-sized gravel). This is best placed under the eaves and should run to a convenient ditch, or a least well away from the building.

Protect the base of the wall from 'rain-splash' and wind scour. This may be by rendering or surface coating (see F2) or by stabilization (see A4). Whitewash the base where termites are found (see C4).

Standard

Where there is a risk of water penetration, rammed earth walls shall be constructed so as to prevent moisture from the ground transmitting up and into the building.

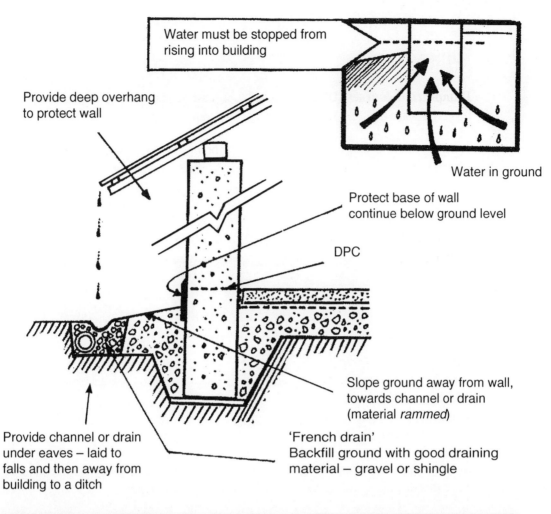

Water must be stopped from rising into building

Water in ground

Provide deep overhang to protect wall

Protect base of wall continue below ground level

DPC

Slope ground away from wall, towards channel or drain (material *rammed*)

Provide channel or drain under eaves – laid to falls and then away from building to a ditch

'French drain' Backfill ground with good draining material – gravel or shingle

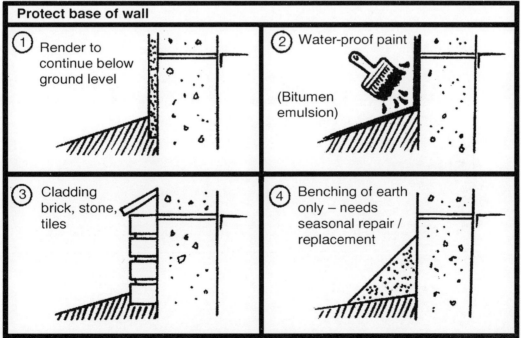

Protect base of wall

① Render to continue below ground level

② Water-proof paint

(Bitumen emulsion)

③ Cladding brick, stone, tiles

④ Benching of earth only – needs seasonal repair / replacement

Rising damp protection to walls

C2: RISING DAMP PROTECTION TO WALLS

C3 FLOORS

Guide

Earth can make a very adequate floor so long as care is taken to achieve good compaction and to avoid water penetration.

Topsoil should be removed, including any visible plant roots from subsoil. The subsoil should be compacted if sandy, or left uncompacted if it contains much clay. Build up stones or hardcore to a compact and flat level. Hardcore should be finished smooth by adding a layer of sandy material.

Compaction of floors should be done by hand or mechanically, using air rammer or vibrating plate. The floor should be built up in layers, maximum 150mm thick, with finer material used towards the surface.

Over large areas it is advisable to set out the floor in bays (3m wide) using timber battens or laying strips of rammed earth 300mm wide. To avoid cracks, shrinkage joints should be left at intervals of about 1.5m, 30mm deep and 6mm wide, which can be filled with earth mortar after the floor has been left to dry.

Where a site is likely to have rising damp, this should be prevented from rising to the floor by means of a **damp-proof membrane**.

Damp-proofing can be provided by a polythene sheet or applied soft bitumen (ideally 3mm thick) or three coats of bitumen solution, bitumen/rubber emulsion or tar/rubber emulsion (ideally 3mm thick).

The DPM should be at least 150mm above the highest level of adjoining ground. If the DPM is laid above any part of the earth floor, then the earth needs to be stabilized to the same standard as foundations. In areas of high rainfall, raise DPM to 300mm above ground level.

Finishing will depend on what the floor is to be used for, the standard needed and the local customs for cleaning and maintenance. Options include:

- well compacted earth;
- sand (kept clean by raking regularly);
- sand cement screed;
- local natural oil mixed with top layer (e.g. soya, linseed);
- lino paint plus hard wax polish;
- pre-case earth block tiles;
- terratile.

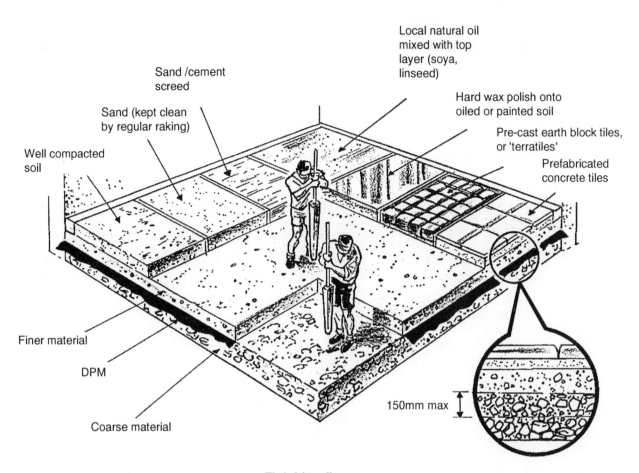

Local natural oil mixed with top layer (soya, linseed)

Sand /cement screed

Hard wax polish onto oiled or painted soil

Sand (kept clean by regular raking)

Pre-cast earth block tiles, or 'terratiles'

Well compacted soil

Prefabricated concrete tiles

Finer material

DPM

Coarse material

150mm max

Finishing floors

PART C: GROUNDWORKS

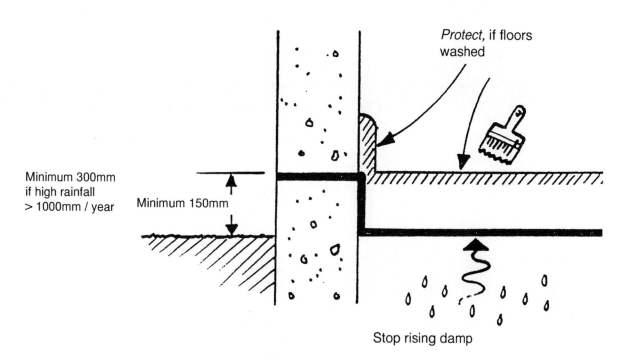

Minimum 300mm
if high rainfall
> 1000mm / year

Minimum 150mm

Protect, if floors washed

Stop rising damp

Damp protection for floors

C4 TERMITE RESISTANCE

Guide

> Note: the wall itself is not at any risk, but it may act as a pathway to timbers in the building.

There are two types of **termite**:

- o the **drywood** termites which need no ground contact, and can fly into the roof or elsewhere. The colony or nest may be developed inside timber members, and will remain unseen until major damage has already occurred;

- o the **subterranean** termites which are much more numerous in terms of species, and need ground contact. Their nests will be either underground or in their above-ground constructions.

All structural timbers should be of termite-resistant material, or impregnated with a termite toxin or repellant. This is especially important in the case of wall plates where these are being used as ring-beams in earthquake areas. A list of naturally resistant timbers is given at the end of this section.

If treatment can be carried out within one week of felling, then Boron infusion will be economical and effective. This may be at a licensed sawmill, using 'Timbor' (TM). Alternatively, an infusion treatment kit may be set up at the felling site, provided there is proper supervision. Sodium borate salt at 4.5kg/m^3 of timber is used, and gives protection against many varieties of rot and wood-destroying insects (such as powder post beetle). Protection from weather is needed.

All treated timbers must be retreated if cut after treatment, except if infusion has been used.

In addition, a '**termite proof course**' can be established throughout the ground slab/wall base level, using material impassable to locally found species. This may be (only the first suitable in earthquake areas):

- • stabilized soil, minimum 5% OPC   100mm
- • bitumen layer   3mm
- • wood tar   3mm
- • ground glass, minimum 10%   100mm
- • metal sheet (projected 50mm)   1mm

Careful attention to **design of joinery items** is sensible. It pays to use metal details where practical. PVC has also been suggested, but this will need to be of high quality to avoid solar degradation from ultra-violet rays.

Subsoil poison treatments of surrounding ground and below building are expensive and have a limited life, depending on soil type and climate.

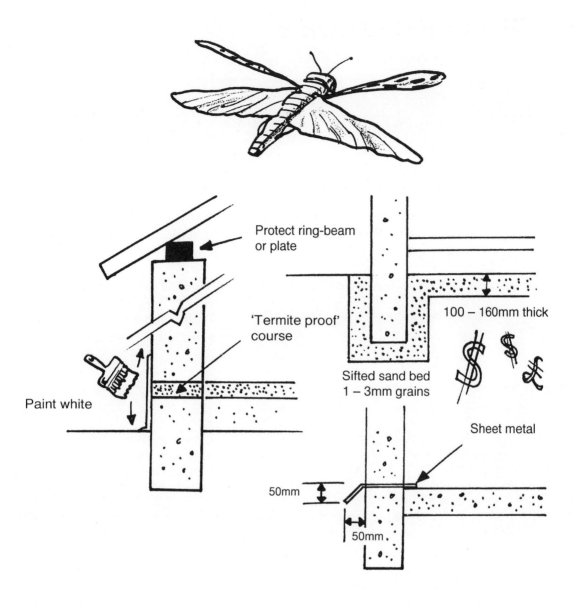

Protect ring-beam or plate

'Termite proof' course

Paint white

100 – 160mm thick

Sifted sand bed 1 – 3mm grains

Sheet metal

50mm

50mm

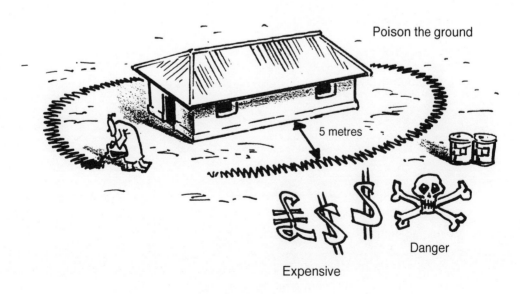

Poison the ground

5 metres

Expensive

Danger

Termite resistance

C4: TERMITE RESISTANCE

There are four main types of chemical in use:

- o organochlorines (OC): very effective protection at concentrations of 0.5% to 1%, but because of environmental fears have been banned in USA, and elsewhere have often been banned or withdrawn, and are not recommended;

- o organophosphorus (OP): needs 2% concentration and is then very effective in humid conditions; does not perform well in hot dry conditions (see map);

- o synthetic pyrethroids: very effective at 1% concentration, but being newer their life is not known; may not last beyond six to ten years. Perform best in hot, dry climates;

- o boron: disodium octaborate or borax at minimum 2%; will dissolve if high groundwater level, but very low environmental risks. Low solubility boron is in development stage.

Biological control is under research, but no effective vector has yet been found.

A sifted sand-bed, where all the grains are between 1mm and 3mm, cannot be penetrated by termites which use their jaws for tunnelling; a barrier under a building and around the outside must be 100–160mm thick. Obtaining such sand would usually be costly, however.

Insecticidal baits are being studied: they might use a thousand-fold less insecticide than ordinary soil treatment.

Note: underground termites are very persistent in searching for their food (wood, straw and other organic materials). When they find a barrier, they will try to find a way round it. This will often be by way of a tunnel built on the surface of a wall. Such tunnels can be easily removed if noticed, so it is useful to paint walls white, especially near the ground. Always remove these termite tunnels as soon as they are seen.

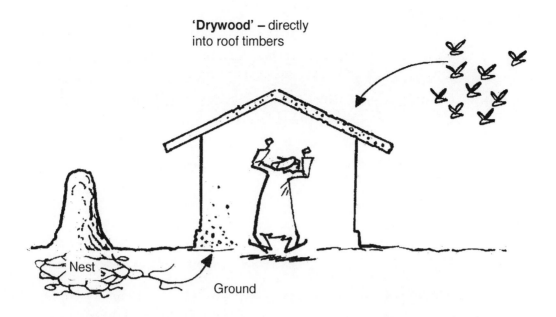

'Drywood' – directly into roof timbers

Nest

Ground

Subterranean – will explore, and bore through walls to find wood

Termites

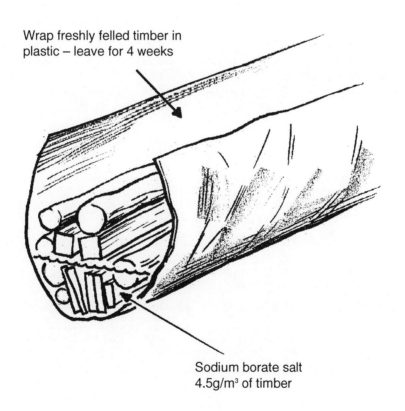

Wrap freshly felled timber in plastic – leave for 4 weeks

Sodium borate salt 4.5g/m³ of timber

Timber treatment

Standard

Rammed earth structures shall be constructed so as to reduce the risk of long-term infestation by termites.

The following timbers are naturally resistant to termite attack. Heartwood should be used in all cases.

Scientific family name	Trees in this family
• Ochnacease	Ekki (kaku)
• Guttiferae	African apple
• Humiriacease	Tiabutuo
• Caesalpiniaceae	
Afzelia africana	Papao
Bussea occidentalis	Samanta
• Mimosacease	Ovala
(except Albizia)	Dahoma
	Okan (denya)
• Papilionacease	
Afrormosia Elata	Afrormosia (kokrodua)
Pterocarpus erinaceus	Senegal rosewood
• Moraceae, but only	
Morus mesozygia	Wonton
Chlorophora excelsa	Iroko (odum)
• Olaceae	
Ongokea gore	Bodwe
• Sapindaceae	Akee apple (akye)
• Sapotaceae	
Gluema ivorensis	Nsudua
Manilkara multinervis	Berekankum
• Palmae (not a true wood)	
Borassus aethiopum	Agobeam
Elaeis guineensis	Oil palm

Note: termite resistance of other species may be locally known. In some cases, the resistance will vary according to sex of tree.

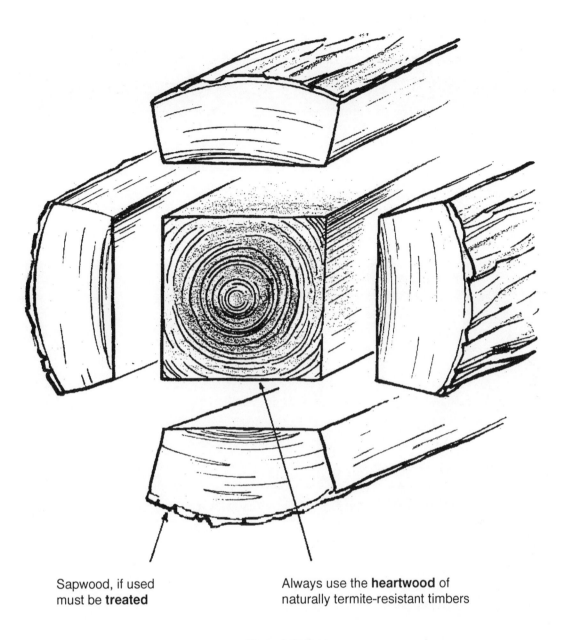

Sapwood, if used
must be **treated**

Always use the **heartwood** of
naturally termite-resistant timbers

Use of timber

Part D: Superstructure

D1 COMPRESSIVE STRENGTH OF WALLS

Guide

Rammed earth can achieve high levels of compressive strength, usually without the need for stabilization. In some cases it may be necessary to adjust the mix of materials in the earth. Too much clay in the soil will increase its compressibility, too little will prevent it binding. In some cases it may be necessary to add stabilization to the soil (A2).

An important factor in achieving the maximum possible compressive strength is ensuring the maximum dry density in the material. This is controlled by obtaining the Ideal Water Content (see A3).

Test N/2, the 'drop' test, should be repeated whenever there is a new soil source, or a new work-gang, or change of weather.

Other factors in improving good strength are ensuring that the initial material is well mixed (see A4) and that good ramming and formwork techniques are used (see Part B).

Standard

Rammed earth walls shall be tested for compressive strength. The average compressive strength shall not be less than 1.5N/mm² generally, or 2.0N/mm² for walls of height between 3.0m and 6.0m

TEST N/4 : 'COMPRESSIVE STRENGTH'

[See also Test N/4 : 'Test cube']

Purpose

To apply a compressive stress to the wall equal to the Standard. If the wall is unmarked at least eight times out ten, it will have complied.

Step one:

Select the spring tension needed to give the compressive stress which the wall must bear: 1.5N/mm² for one-storey walls of up to 400mm thick and 3.0N/mm² for two-storey walls, at minimum age of seven days.

Step two:

Place the face of the spring firmly against the wall to be tested – ideally a top surface, but can be the wall face. Then gently but firmly push the tester towards the wall until the flat plate is touching the wall face, and remove the tester.

Step three:

Examine the wall. No depression should show where the force was applied. If it does, the wall has failed the test; it must pass at least eight times out of ten.

PART D: SUPERSTRUCTURE

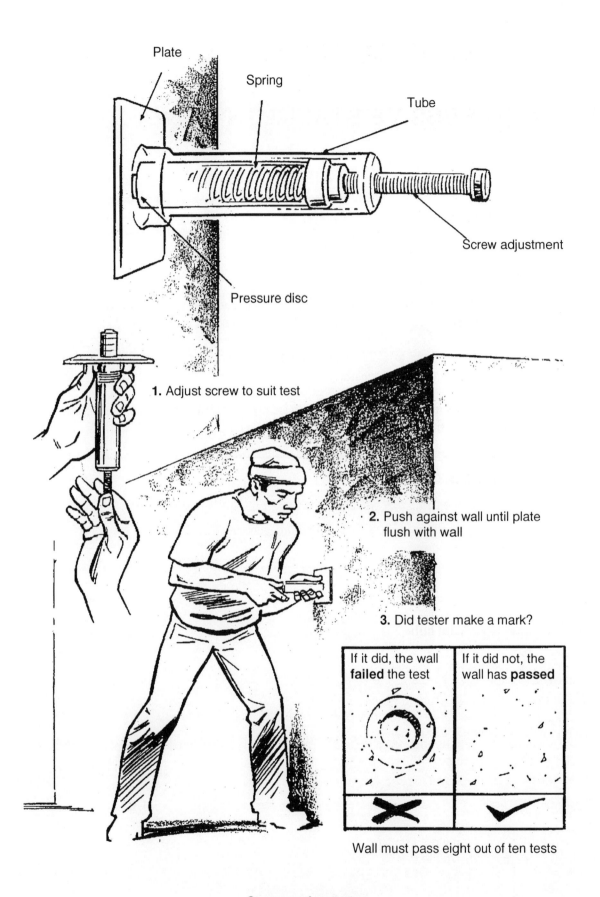

Plate

Spring

Tube

Screw adjustment

Pressure disc

1. Adjust screw to suit test

2. Push against wall until plate flush with wall

3. Did tester make a mark?

If it did, the wall **failed** the test	If it did not, the wall has **passed**
✗	✓

Wall must pass eight out of ten tests

Compression tester

D1: COMPREHENSIVE STRENGTH OF WALLS

D2 DENSITY OF WALLS

Guide

The **density** of the material is an important indicator of the strength and durability of the finished wall. Maximum dry density is achieved when the material rammed is at Ideal Water Content (IWC – see A3).

Density requirement assumes normal dense aggregates. Aerated material such as pumice (volcanic material) would not achieve the density standard, though its strength might be adequate when tested for compression.

Standard

The specific density of rammed earth walls shall be:

Wet [within eight hours of being rammed]:	Dry [after 28 days]:
1850kg/m^3 minimum	1800 kg/m^3 minimum
2100kg/m^3 recommended	2000 kg/m^3 recommended

TEST N/4 : 'TEST CUBE'

[Alternative to Test N/4 : 'Compressive strength' – one or other of these tests must be performed.]

Purpose

To find the density of a sample block made from the same material and in the same way as the walls being built.

Step one:

Make three test cubes from the material used for ramming using a mould 150mm high x 150mm long x 150mm thick (a standard concrete test cube mould) which has been oiled for easy release. Compact the material by placing a hardwood block 147 x 147mm face on 100mm of the soil (loose) and give eighteen heavy blows using a 7.5kg rammer. Repeat three times (an extension to the mould will be needed for the third layer), then smooth the top surface and remove from the mould. Leave this block to cure for 28 days.

Step two:

After 28 days crush the sample blocks and then dry this material without heating it over 30°C. (Heating can affect the result by removing water bonded to soil particles.) Make sure that none of the material is lost when it is crushed.

Step three:

Weigh the material. Repeat steps two and three until the weight lost in one cycle is not more than 0.05kg.

Step four:

Work out the density as follows:

$$\text{Density in kg/m}^3 = \frac{\text{dry weight of material (kg)}}{\text{volume (m}^3\text{)}}$$

where volume = 0.003375 for the 150mm cube.

The average density of the three blocks should be no less than the standard.

PART D: SUPERSTRUCTURE

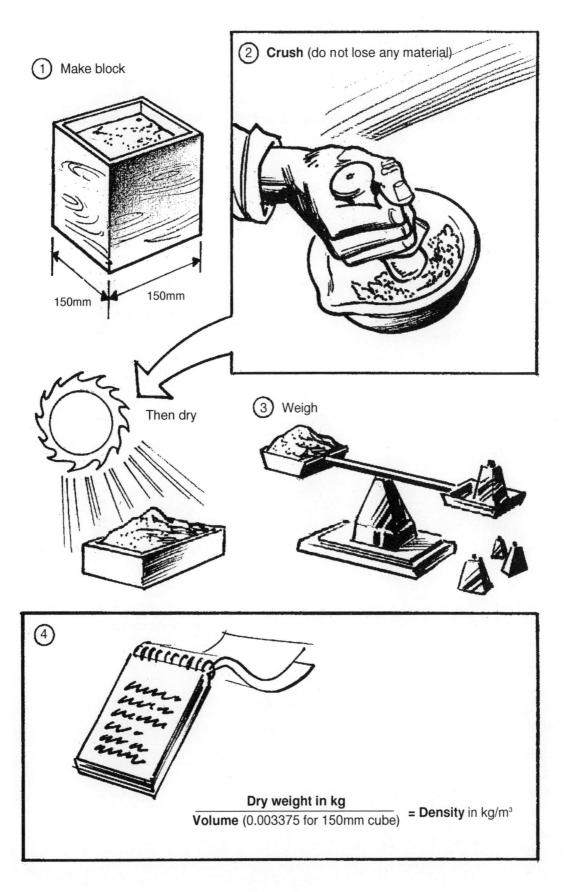

① Make block

150mm 150mm

② **Crush** (do not lose any material)

Then dry

③ Weigh

④

$$\frac{\textbf{Dry weight in kg}}{\textbf{Volume} \text{ (0.003375 for 150mm cube)}} = \textbf{Density in kg/m}^3$$

'Test cube'

D3 WATER ABSORPTION OF WALLS

Guide

The effect of water on earth walls is to break the bonds between particles, thus lowering crushing strength. Protection from water absorption is important for the durability of the wall. Wherever groundwater may occur (even if infrequently) then protection at the base must be given by a damp-proof course (see C2). Protection at the top must be given by a roof or capping (see D4).

Water absorption can be lowered by a good mix of soil, good compaction and Ideal Water Content when ramming. Stabilization of the soil can be used to improve poor water absorption results (see A4). An alternative approach is to protect the wall with a surface treatment. Various types of renderings are discussed in more details in F2.

Standard

Walls shall be protected from excessive water absorption at the base, the top, and the face.

Mean annual precipitation

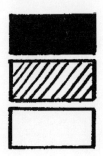

More than 1000mm

200 – 1000mm

Less than 200mm

Rainfall in Africa

D3: WATER ABSORPTION OF WALLS

D4 WEATHER EROSION OF WALLS

Guide

Earth walls may be eroded at their surface by driving rain, which can loosen the smaller particles.

Walls will perform better when a good soil mix is used (see A1) and the soil well compacted (see B2) at Ideal Water Content (see A3).

Always ensure 'a good hat, boots and a coat' for long life.

A good **hat**: walls will be protected by deep overhangs. **This point is very important indeed.** It is a false economy to build only a small overhang. Significant protection will be given to a depth below overhang of three times the projection, where wind conditions are not severe. Of course, the roof itself must not leak.

Boots: the base of walls will be worn by splashback of rain, if not protected. Protection from rain-splash onto the base of the wall, but over the DPC, should be given. This is a vital point, especially for unstabilized soil (see C2). There are two ways of approach:

To provide a resistant surface. This may be given by a render, by using bricks or stone, or by building the lower part of the wall using a stabilizer, even if the upper part will be plain soil.

To add a 'sacrificial' layer, and replace this when it has worn. The cheaper approach of using an extra layer of soil which will be eroded by the rain-splash, and then replaced, is effective **provided it is maintained.**

Coat: the main wall surface can either be coated or built to withstand driving rain. Various types of coatings and renderings are discussed in more detail in F2; stabilization is another approach to poor weather erosion results, which can be dramatically improved (see A4).

It is possible to allow walls with poor erosion standards when a high degree of building maintenance can be expected.

In some areas, **wind scour**, the effect of wind-driven sand particles removing the surface fines (much as driving rain can do), will occur, if no protection is given (see **boots**).

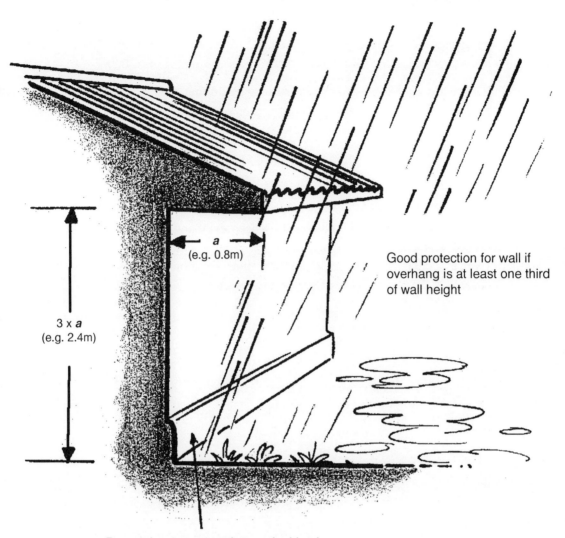

$3 \times a$
(e.g. 2.4m)

a
(e.g. 0.8m)

Good protection for wall if
overhang is at least one third
of wall height

Remember to protect from splashback

Erosion protection for walls

Standard

Rammed earth walls exposed to weather shall be tested (including any surface treatment proposed) using the 'drip' test, and shall remain intact not less than:

- o **2 hours**
  for dry areas with rainfall less than 200mm per year

- o **6 hours**
  for areas with rainfall between 200mm and 1000mm per year

- o **24 hours**
  for areas with rainfall above 1000mm per year

TEST N/5 : 'DRIP' TEST

Purpose

To test how the wall will perform in driving rain.

Step one:

Make a test tile 150 x 150 x 20mm after compaction. (The same mould used for N/4 'Test cube' may be used, with a blockout to reduce the depth of the sample.) Allow the tile to dry naturally. (If the wall is to have a coating or rendering, add such a coating/rendering to the tile in the specified manner, before testing.)

Step two:

Suspend a bucket with two gallons of water in it, and a length of string which has one end immersed in the water (must touch bottom of the bucket) and the other end hanging vertically over the centre of the test cube. The string should be saturated so that a continual flow of drips runs down and onto the block. (Avoid using plastic or nylon string.) The distance between the end of the string and the tile shall be 2.5m. Continue the test for the time specified in the standard.

Step three:

If the tile is intact, it has passed the test. If it has disintegrated, it has failed.

PART D: SUPERSTRUCTURE

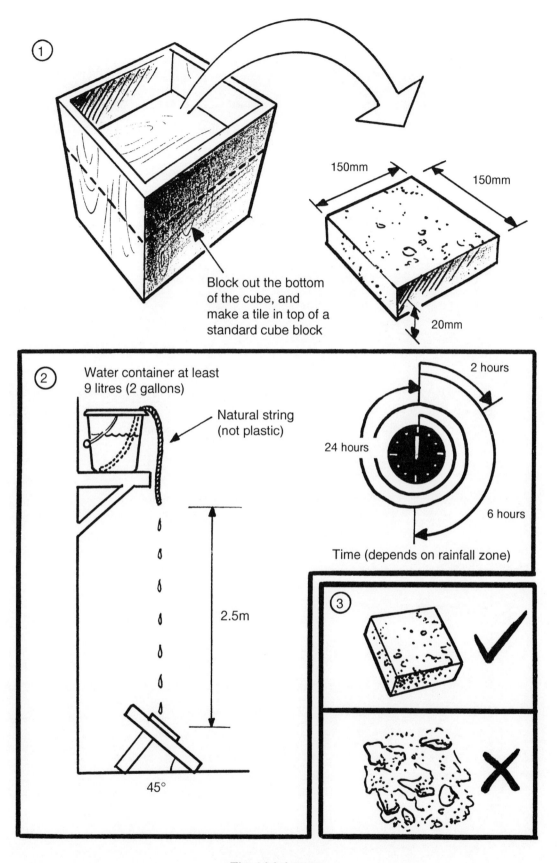

① Block out the bottom of the cube, and make a tile in top of a standard cube block

150mm

150mm

20mm

② Water container at least 9 litres (2 gallons)

Natural string (not plastic)

2 hours

24 hours

6 hours

Time (depends on rainfall zone)

2.5m

45°

③ ✓

✗

The 'drip' test

D5 WALLS : VISUAL TEST

Guide

Corners and exposed edges should be protected from wear either by putting a triangular fill in the formwork – to produce a chamfered corner – or by building up the corner using concrete wedges, or stone/brick.

Honeycombing is caused in a number of ways:

- o oversized gravel next to formwork (work gravel away from sides of formwork using a space, before ramming – this is called 'paddling');
- o poorly mixed soil (mix better);
- o too little clay to permit compaction (change soil mix);
- o water content not correct (too little/too much).

Joint cracks and construction holes should be filled soon after construction, unless it is planned to render the wall, in which case holes will act as 'key' for the render.

Shrinkage cracks may be caused by a high clay content in the soil, and so can be reduced by reducing the clay content; stabilization will also reduce shrinkage. Lime and pozzolana mixtures work well with clay (see A4).

Slow down the drying out of the wall, especially when working in hot, clear sunshine:

- o keep the wall surface damp by lightly spraying with water;
- o shade the wall, for example, use plaited grass or palm leaf screens.

This applies to new rendering too.

Standard

Walls shall be free of broken edges and honeycombing.

Joint cracks, construction holes and holes caused by striking formwork shall be filled using compatible material within 24 hours of their appearance, or the wall rendered.

Shrinkage cracks shall not be more than 3mm wide and 75mm in length, and be limited to twenty in any square metre. All shrinkage cracks shall be made good or the wall rendered

---

Honeycombing
- Paddle gravel away
- Mix soil better
- Add clay
- Check water content

Joint cracks and construction holes
- Fill

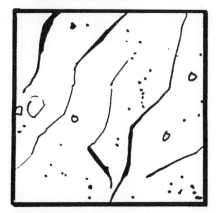

Shrinkage cracks
- Improve mix
- Stabilize
- Render

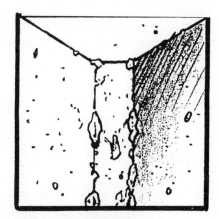

Corners crumbling
- Add fillet in formwork to produce chamfer
- Build corners in brick or concrete brick or concrete

Sun screen

Dampen wall to slow down drying

Repair damage to walls

Part E: Stability

E1 STABILITY OF WALLS : SLENDERNESS

Guide

Cement stabilized rammed earth can be built with higher ratios (thinner walls) because they can resist bending forces to a slightly greater extent.

Because ramming often takes place with a man standing between the two sides of the formwork, a minimum wall width of 300mm is convenient.

In areas of medium or high seismicity (where earthquakes may be expected) more rigorous standards should be achieved (see G1).

Standard

The slenderness ratios for rammed earth walls shall meet the limits in Table E1, and in no case shall walls be less then 230mm thick.

Table E1 Slenderness ratios for rammed earth walls

Maximum length	Restraint	Stabilized	Ratio (width:height)
9m	unrestrained	unstabilized	1:8
9m	unrestrained	cement stabilized	1:10
9m	restrained	unstabilized	1:12
9m	restrained	cement stabilized	1:16

A 'restrained' wall is one that is at least bonded by lapping alternate courses to a return wall and/or pier of not less than 450mm length, at both ends; or better where the return wall is built continuously with it.

Walls may be stepped in as they rise in height, provided that the slenderness ratio for the wall above still meets Table E1.

Exemption: such other dimensions as the building supervisor may approve.

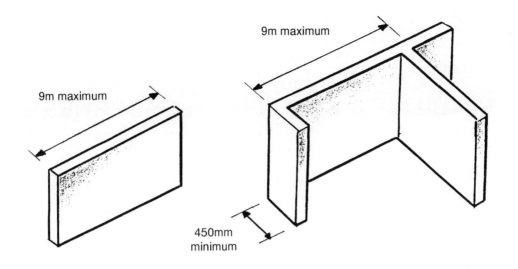

Unrestrained
Unstabilized 1 : 8
Stabilized 1 : 10

Restrained
Unstabilized 1 : 12
Stabilized 1 : 16

Wall may step in e.g. for unrestrained, unstabilized

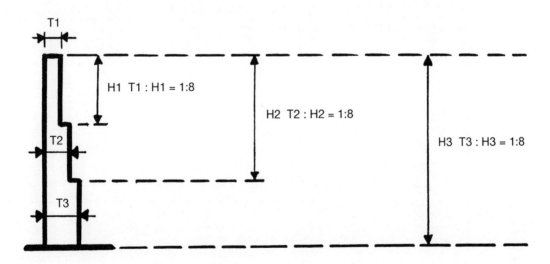

H1 T1 : H1 = 1:8

H2 T2 : H2 = 1:8

H3 T3 : H3 = 1:8

Stability of walls

E1: STABILITY OF WALLS: SLENDERNESS

E2 STABILITY OF WALLS : OPENINGS AND LINTELS

Guide

Openings will weaken the wall in which they are placed, and will need to support any loads placed on top of them. This guide first discusses what materials may be used **over** the opening, then adds general construction points.

Timber lintels. The size of timber required for openings depends on the species and standard of timber. Follow local custom and codes. Timber lintels should be protected from attack from both water (leading to rot), wood boring insect and termite attack – if the species is not naturally resistant (see C4).

Reinforced earth lintels (RE lintels). RE lintels may be formed integrally with the rammed walls. Reinforcement must be as described in the 'deemed to satisfy' section overleaf if the opening is not more than 1000mm; cement is needed in this case. Bars should be covered (minimum 30mm). But do not try to precast RE lintels as they are likely to crack when moved.

Reinforced concrete lintels (RC lintels). RC lintels can either be prefabricated or poured on site. Care should be taken to ensure adequate reinforcement, and that the reinforcement bars are sufficiently covered (minimum 25mm). Bars must be secured in place at the time of pouring concrete.

Arches. Unreinforced arches can be used successfully in earth walls, so long as they comply with the 'deemed to satisfy' provisions. Arches help in the transfer of loads. Avoiding steel also avoids the risk of rust in humid areas.

If span exceeds 1000mm, lintels or arches should be calculated in accordance with local codes.

Openings can be planned outside the limits of the 'deemed to satisfy' clause if it can be shown that the wall is still stable.

Generally, it is the unbuttressed piers between openings that are the weak points; these piers can be reinforced or upgraded with stabilization. Reinforcement in the wall over and near openings will improve the stability and help strengthen the piers and corners.

Ensure that lintels have sufficient bearing each end (200mm required).

Ensure that load from roof trusses, beams or rafters is always spread by a plate (timber, steel or concrete).

In areas of medium or high seismicity, higher standards apply (see G1).

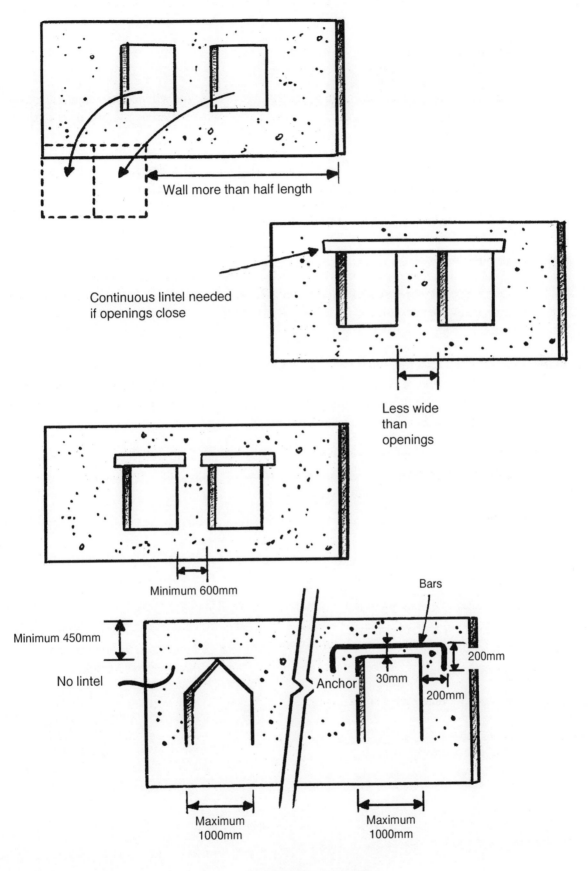

Wall more than half length

Continuous lintel needed
if openings close

Less wide
than
openings

Minimum 600mm

Minimum 450mm

No lintel

Bars

200mm

30mm

Anchor

200mm

Maximum
1000mm

Maximum
1000mm

Openings and lintels

E: STABILITY OF WALLS: OPENINGS AND LINTELS

Deemed to satisfy

Openings in any wall shall not constitute more than one half of the length of the wall, and, where groups of doors or windows are of less distance apart than the width of the openings, lintels shall be made continuous over the series.

Minimum distance of 600mm between openings with separate lintels.

No lintel is required if:

- o   there is no wall over the opening (opening reaches plate);
- o   the head is arched (circular or pointed):
  - with minimum 450mm of wall above the crown;
  - openings are limited to 1000mm wide;
  - the rise from the base to the crown of the arch (whether pointed or curved) is not less than half of the opening width;
  - care is taken in formwork to support ramming loads (usually a 'blockout' will be needed – see Part B).

Flat headed 'arch' openings not wider than 1000mm may be built in areas of low or medium rainfall using 6mm steel bars in stabilized earth at minimum 100mm centres and 30mm cover: bars to extend minimum 200mm beyond opening, and to be anchored at each end.

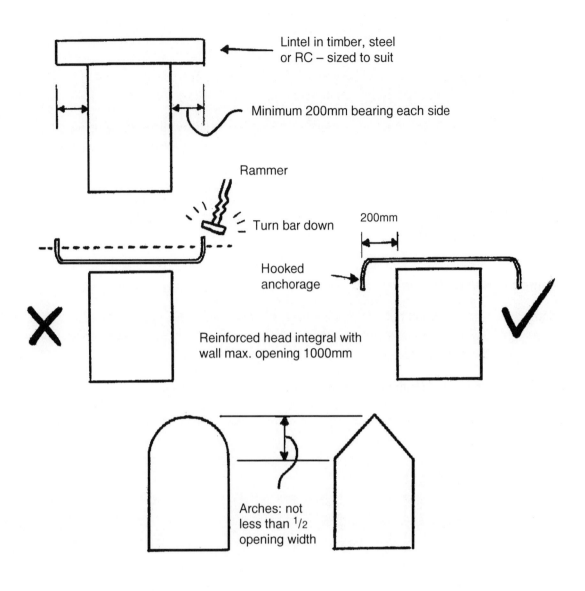

Lintel in timber, steel or RC – sized to suit

Minimum 200mm bearing each side

Rammer

Turn bar down

Hooked anchorage

200mm

Reinforced head integral with wall max. opening 1000mm

Arches: not less than $1/2$ opening width

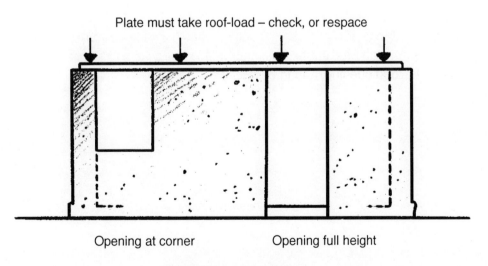

Plate must take roof-load – check, or respace

Opening at corner

Opening full height

(If restrained at roof level)

Requirements for openings

E2: STABILITY OF WALLS: OPENINGS AND LINTELS

E3 STABILITY OF WALLS : BONDING

Guide

There are two ways to move formwork: sideways and upwards (see Part B). The way to bond sections of wall together will depend partly on which formwork method is to be used.

Sideways movement of formwork normally requires bonded joints similar to block or brick masonry walling; think of each 'cast' (one form fully rammed) as a very large brick. The weakest point will be at the corner where the overlap will be limited to the wall thickness – this is why formwork which permits corners to be rammed in one piece is recommended.

Round the corner formwork will improve the bonding at corners, but remember that the 'L-shaped' form needed for this must allow one longer and one shorter leg, so that the next course can be reversed to give an overlapping bond.

Upwards movement of formwork requires a positive interlocking joint between each panel, with at least 25mm, but preferably 50mm, offsets or rebates.

Internal walls should be bonded to external walls or piers.

Good bonding is particularly important in areas of medium or high seismicity (see G1).

Standard

Rammed earth walls shall be built so that the individual sections of wall bond with the rest of the wall by staggering joints not less than the thickness of the wall.

Exemption: vertical joints in wall sections are permitted if:

o   foundations are in reinforced concrete

o   or if adjacent sections interlock on plan by minimum 25mm.

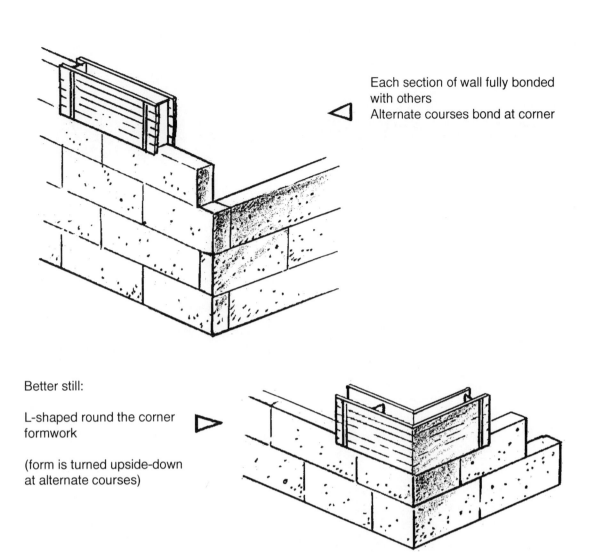

Each section of wall fully bonded with others
Alternate courses bond at corner

Better still:

L-shaped round the corner formwork

(form is turned upside-down at alternate courses)

Interlock examples for rising forms

Filled from top

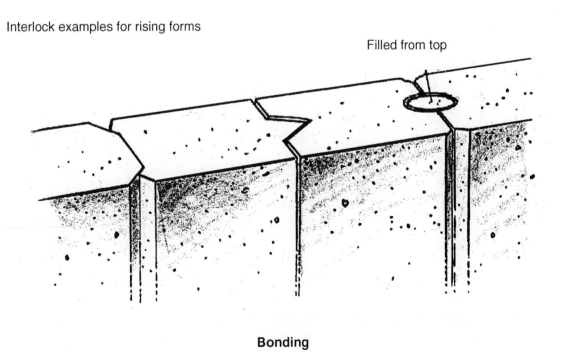

Bonding

E3: STABILITY OF WALLS: BONDING

91

Part F: Details and finishes

F1 FIXINGS AND TIES

Guide

Holes can be made in rammed earth.

Where the roof is lightweight, wind uplift may be greater than the roof weight, so fixing down the roof members is important. The ties need to be well buried in the wall, making use of the wall weight.

Good detailing in joinery avoids many problems. Avoid doors and windows pivoting on a corner of the wall and thus straining the hinges: if doors and windows are mounted either at or on the face of the wall they will have less risk of damage. Alternatively, door, shutter or window stops may be provided. The use of standard frame anchors is quite satisfactory.

The use of metal fixed frames will help in securing moving parts, and will not be attacked by termites; doors and windows in constant use should also be free from attack.

An alternative to metal frames is the use of metal hinges inserted directly into the wall, which, if carefully done, can avoid the need for a frame altogether.

When using metal items, consider the local climate. Will the metal rust? Should it be protected by galvanizing or paint? What grade of metal is available? (some steels are soft or brittle).

Standard

Roofs must be anchored to secure them against the wind forces to be expected.

Large items of joinery, such as doors and windows, and other heavy objects to be fixed to rammed earth walls, shall be fixed securely and in such a way as not to damage the wall.

Deemed to satisfy

Roof frame and/or wall plates (or timber ring-beams) shall be anchored at 900mm centres using:

- o two strands of eight gauge minimum galvanized wire, secured to plates and built 450mm minimum depth into wall, using 150mm long anchor at bottom;

- o one galvanized or non-ferrous metal strip, minimum 25 x 2mm, secured to plates and built into wall 450mm minimum, using 150mm long anchor at bottom.

Such other anchor as the building supervisor shall approve.

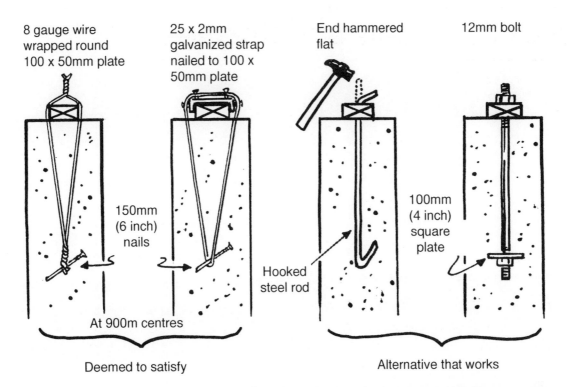

8 gauge wire wrapped round 100 x 50mm plate

25 x 2mm galvanized strap nailed to 100 x 50mm plate

End hammered flat

12mm bolt

150mm (6 inch) nails

Hooked steel rod

100mm (4 inch) square plate

At 900m centres

Deemed to satisfy

Alternative that works

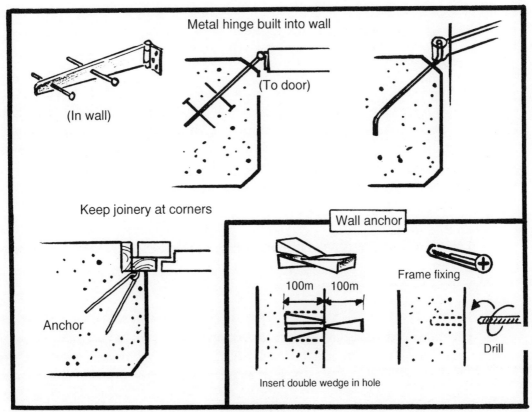

Metal hinge built into wall

(In wall)

(To door)

Keep joinery at corners

Wall anchor

Anchor

100m   100m

Frame fixing

Drill

Insert double wedge in hole

Fixings

F1: FIXINGS

F2 SURFACE TREATMENTS

Guide

Most earth walls, even stabilized walls, may benefit from surface treatments. Renders may be used externally or internally. The reasons for adding a surface can be any of the following:

- waterproofing;
- resistance to wear;
- reduction in vermin hiding places, thus improved health;
- reduced maintenance;
- reduction in heat-gain by reflection;
- ease of surface cleaning;
- improved appearance.

Reasons against adding a surface include:

- extra cost (acceptance of continuing maintenance);
- suitable materials not available;
- process is more complicated (skills not available).

Rammed earth walls, if well made, can withstand a certain amount of rain, provided this cannot settle on the top of any surface (such as cills). However, with time, the smallest particles will be washed out, leaving a roughened surface. With ideal soil and good workmanship such a wall will last indefinitely, but otherwise further wear will follow. Thus a surface treatment which will bind the particles in place is useful, but render finishes **are not specifically required** if the finished wall meets the standards without them.

SURFACE FINISHES

Lime-wash (whitewash) has traditionally been used by many builders as a surface finish, and this remains a good solution. The lime-wash will need periodic renewal, ideally each year.

Polymer emulsion (PVA) is a newer product (not emulsion paint, but similar to white wood glue) which can be applied by brush or, better still, by spray – a backpack or stirrup-pump can be used. PVA can be used at a range of different dilutions in water; it is useful in helping adhesion of renders, or may be used as the finishing coat where a transparent coating (exposing the appearance of the soil) is wanted. A solvent-based system of acrylic sealer is recommended for walls facing extremes of wind-driven rain.

Bitumen emulsion, such as road-builders use (e.g. Colas) is another approach (where a painted or 'tyrolean' finish will be applied). This should not be applied when the wall is still in the early stages of drying out, as the bitumen will not adhere and be 'thrown off' the wall surface.

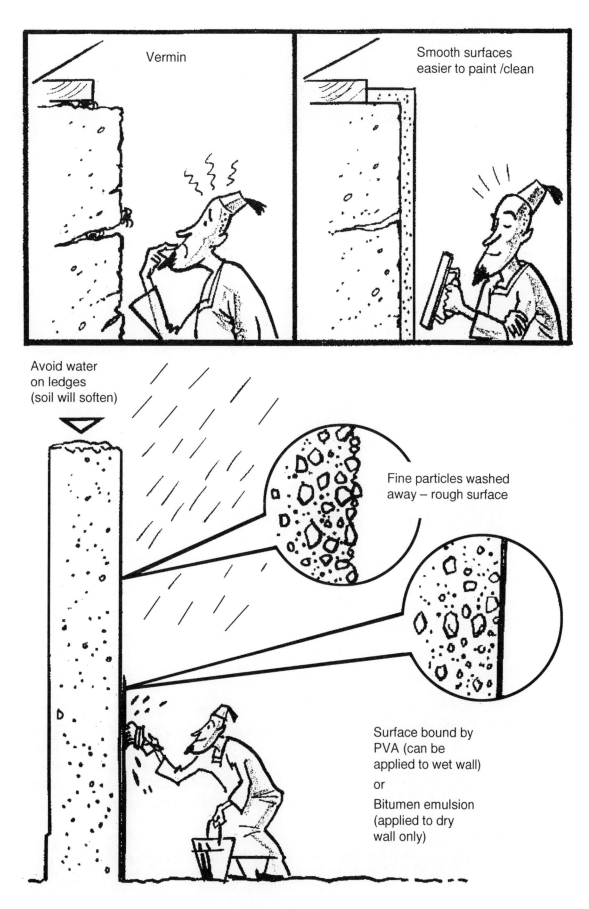

Surface treatments

F2: SURFACE TREATMENTS

Emulsion paint will be absorbed if used alone, but an interesting finish can be given by mixing emulsion paint with sand, which is then 'thrown' over a base coat of bitumen emulsion while the base coat is still tacky.

Oil paint: good practice details when applying oil paint:

- remember that an earth wall will suck in anything soluble;

- penetration of paint is **not** helpful to durability, so avoid primers that penetrate wall;

- wall must be thoroughly dry and brushed with a broom;

- a linseed oil primer is recommended; a cheaper alternative may be soya bean oil, though less is known about this;

- use paint with at least 88% linseed oil in the carrier and which ideally has at least 50% white lead, and no more than 30% zinc oxide in the pigment;

- do not apply thick coats.

RENDERS

Good soil selection and building design can dispense with need for render, or renders can be placed only on the walls which are most exposed to rain and wind erosion. If a render has been well mixed and applied, it will last a very long time; but damage caused by whatever reason should be repaired before it spreads. Poor bonding of render to the wall beneath is the main reason for failures, and thus the need for maintenance later.

Types of render:

- mud plaster ('Dagga' plaster);
- cement/sand;
- cement/lime/soil;
- cement/soil and lime/soil;
- cement and lime slurries;
- lime/pozzolana with sand or soil;
- gypsum/lime and gypsum/lime/sand;
- bitumen/soil (bitumen heated);
- traditional part organic mixes;
- other traditional and modern renders, e.g. soil/sump-oil.

'Dagga' plaster is about three parts of fine sand to one part clay. The material must be sieved so that only fines are used (a fly screen can be the sieve). Where a clay-rich soil is available, two parts sand and one of the soil-fines may be suitable – a trial should be made. The wall must be dampened before being plastered, and a good physical key will be essential to prevent failure. This plaster will not withstand driving rain, and should be painted if it will be thus exposed. Satisfactory for internal room use where not exposed to washing.

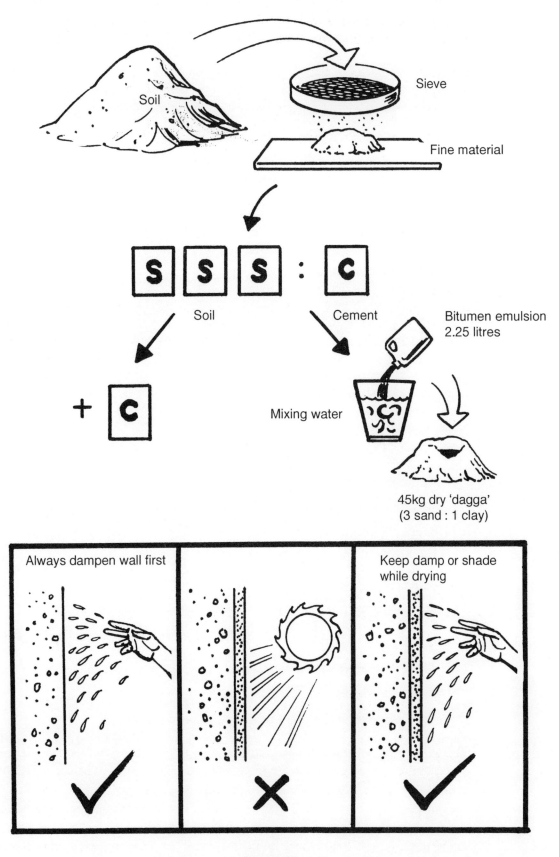

Soil

Sieve

Fine material

S S S : C

Soil

Cement

+ C

Bitumen emulsion
2.25 litres

Mixing water

45kg dry 'dagga'
(3 sand : 1 clay)

Always dampen wall first

Keep damp or shade
while drying

Renders

F2: SURFACE TREATMENTS

Bitumen emulsion, where available, may be added to 'Dagga' plaster by adding to the mixing water at the rate of 2.25 litres/45kg of dry plaster material. This will make a plaster that is much more resistant to driving rain, and thus of good durability – the colour will be darker.

'Dagga' plaster may also be improved by adding cement; the mix should be no stronger than one (cement) to four ('Dagga'); thus 1 : 3 : 1 (cement : sand : clay).

Cement sand render ('stucco') must not be used too strong: 3.5 to 4 parts of sand to one of cement. Again the wall must be dampened to prevent the mix from having the moisture withdrawn from it. Again, too, a good physical bond must be given. The ideal will be an expanded metal mesh, but usually this will cost too much. Nails driven into the walls so that their heads are within the render have proved satisfactory; at the least, the wall should be roughened by pick marks, and should have all loose material brushed off before being rendered. The render must not dry too quickly, and should be shaded and/or sprayed to prevent this. Application as a 'tyrolean' render is recommended; a float can be applied to give a smoother finish where wanted.

Lime, where available, will be a very useful addition; it will soften the render and improve the bond to the wall below. A typical mix would be one (cement) : two (lime) : nine (sand). Where soil is used in place of sand, it must be sieved (only the fines will be used); if it is clay-rich, lime will be better than cement as a hardener. Lime takes much longer than cement to harden, which is useful in the long run.

Good practical details to help renders stay put:

- use renders that are compatible with the wall sub-base. A clay-rich wall will make a poor base for rendering;
- sieved fines from the soil being used, mixed with cement/lime, is recommended for stucco finishes;
- softer renders have better chance of survival and repair;
- if hard renders are required, build up in layers, gradually increasing cement content;
- provide key such as nails, wire, expanded metal and grooved surfaces;
- tyrolean application of the various renders has proved economical and successful.

Other facings: where a wall will be severely exposed, or to protect the base of the wall, other harder facings may be considered, such as burnt bricks, cement or burnt tiles, slates or stone – if these are available (see D4).

Where there is a live local tradition of using other materials – including organic products – to produce successful renders, this is permissible.

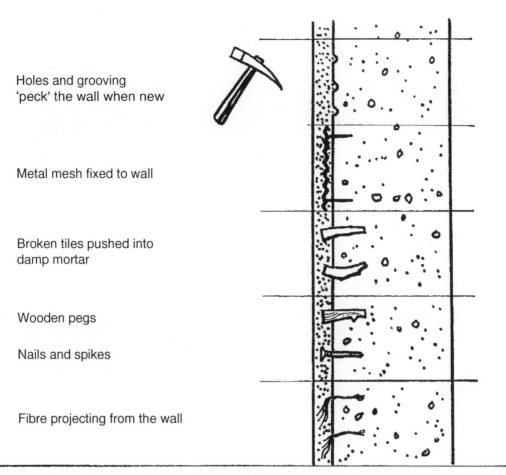

Holes and grooving 'peck' the wall when new

Metal mesh fixed to wall

Broken tiles pushed into damp mortar

Wooden pegs

Nails and spikes

Fibre projecting from the wall

Providing a good key

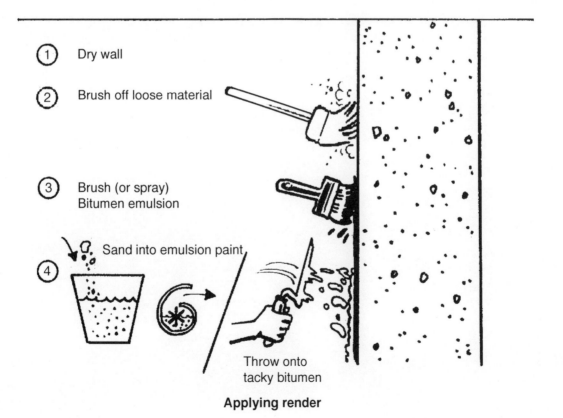

1. Dry wall

2. Brush off loose material

3. Brush (or spray) Bitumen emulsion

4. Sand into emulsion paint

Throw onto tacky bitumen

Applying render

F2: SURFACE TREATMENTS

TEST O/11 : 'RENDER ADHESION'

Purpose

To find out the force needed to pull a rendered surface off the wall beneath it.

Step one:

Prepare an area of wall by applying the proposed rendered surface; deeply score the wet render round a 150mm x 150mm flat plate.

Step two:

When the render (and the wall below) is fully dry, attach the flat plate to the render face using an epoxy-based glue; tie a stout string to the face of the plate, and pass this over a pulley wheel.

Step three:

Place a pan of known weight onto the string; then add quarter-kilogram weights into the pan, allowing ten minutes between each. Note the weight at which the plate pulls the rendered square off the wall face, and note also how much of the wall comes off.

If only the render comes away from the wall, leaving the wall face largely unmarked, there is a poor bond with the wall. If there is as much wall as render pulled away, there is good adhesion. The weight needed to pull the plate away should be greater than 2kg.

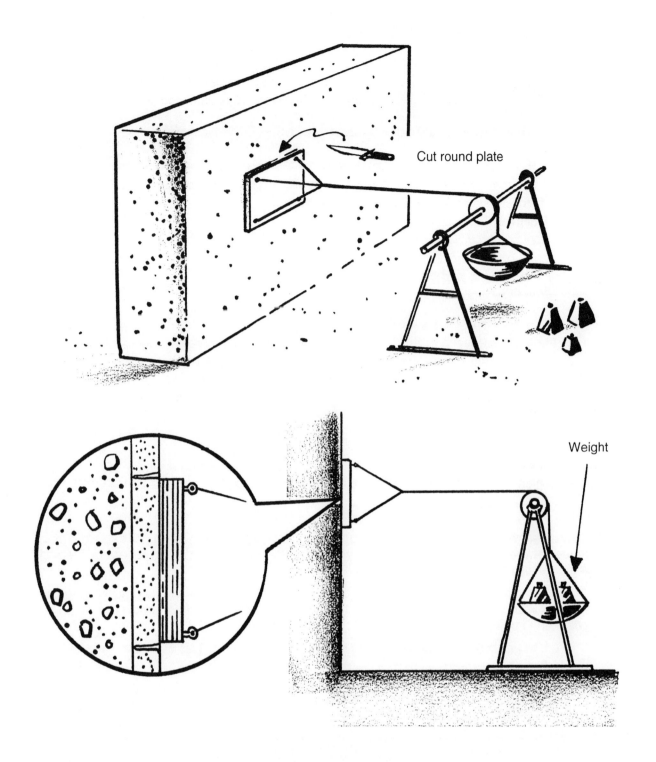

Cut round plate

Weight

'Render adhesion' test

F2: SURFACE TREATMENTS

F3 SERVICE INSERTS

Guide

Think where pipes and wires will be needed before starting to build.

Foul drains and water supply pipes should enter below ground, but above foundation level. Either place a blockout which (after removal) will provide the hole needed, or cut the hole soon after the wall is built (before it has hardened).

When filling around service pipes that enter below ground, make sure that the fill material is as sound as the wall or slab, and using compatible material. A strong cement mix in a soft wall will produce a crack, allowing termites to enter. Bitumen sealants, if available, will be useful.

Electric supply cables, usually coming by overhead lines on poles, are best attached to roof structures (trusses, purlins) and should not be fixed to earth walls unless an anchorage spreading the tension pull of the cable has been built in. Since the cable will swing in the wind, it should be held clear of the wall and not be allowed to scrape the surface.

Electric conduits for light switches and sockets may be run in the centre of the wall down to the outlet point; lightly fix a small blockout to the face of the formwork to help in locating the conduit, and for fixing or recessing the switch or socket.

Standard

Holes through walls made for service inserts for drainage, water, electricity or other services shall not be wider than 300mm, or be provided with lintels as in E2.

Service cables shall not be anchored to rammed earth walls without providing for tension forces.

Vertical or horizontal service ducts (conduits) may only be inserted in the central third of the wall thickness and shall not exceed 10% of that thickness.

Holes entering the house below DPC shall be filled so as to prevent the entry of vermin, insects, or termites.

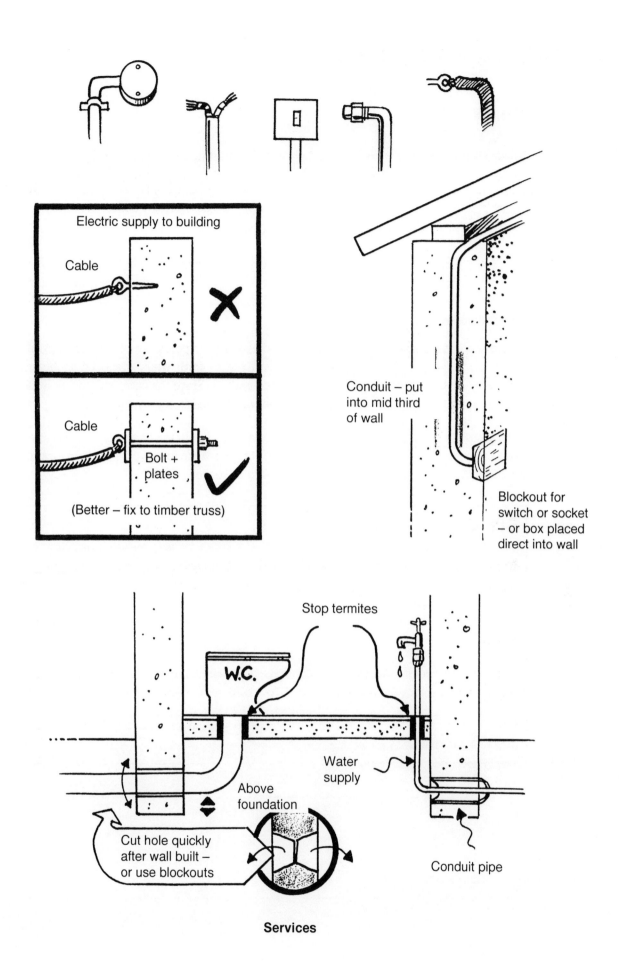

Electric supply to building

Cable

✗

Cable

Bolt + plates

✓

(Better – fix to timber truss)

Conduit – put into mid third of wall

Blockout for switch or socket – or box placed direct into wall

Stop termites

W.C.

Water supply

Above foundation

Cut hole quickly after wall built – or use blockouts

Conduit pipe

Services

F3: SURFACE INSERTS

103

F4 WALLS, FLOORS AND HEALTH

Guide

Studies have shown the importance of reducing the hiding places where disease-carrying pests can live. This is because most predators rest during the day and are active at night when they move out to seek their human hosts. Flea-larvae, house-dust mites, ticks, cockroaches, and a variety of bugs all hide in cracks which they find in walls and floors, so it is important that these should be carefully sealed.

The requirements of D5 (to seal cracks and honeycombing in walls) are necessary, but of equal importance will be the sealing of cracks between door and window frames, especially if these are small – if a crack is large enough to allow a draught through it, it will be less restful to predators.

Some surface materials seem to give a smooth finish and so be suitable, but are liable to peel or crack at their edges. Wallpaper, for instance, should be avoided.

Hollow metal frames (such as the typical louvre window section) should be carefully sealed or filled for the same reasons. On the other hand, the avoidance of door frames altogether (as mentioned in F1) will avoid the possibility of cracks behind frames, and so have an extra benefit.

Floors should be easy to clean so as to encourage the disturbance of resting pests. Make sure that in complying with C3 all joints are filled.

The long-term control of mosquito populations is often by way of wall spraying: the mosquitoes are then infected through their feet. The frequency of spraying needed will depend significantly on the density/absorption of the wall surface. Thus, reaching or exceeding the standard set in D2 will be helpful, since the denser the surface, the longer the effectiveness of a spray will be, perhaps permitting a reduction in the need to spray to once a year.

The digging of earth for rammed earth construction should be done so as to avoid creating pools of stagnant water. Even very shallow pools can create a breeding ground for mosquitoes that, in some cases, will complete their life cycle in only seven days.

When planning the building work, remember that good ventilation will help, provided that mosquitoes cannot enter the building at eaves level.

Standard

Walls and floors should be constructed to avoid providing resting places for insect and arthropod predators.

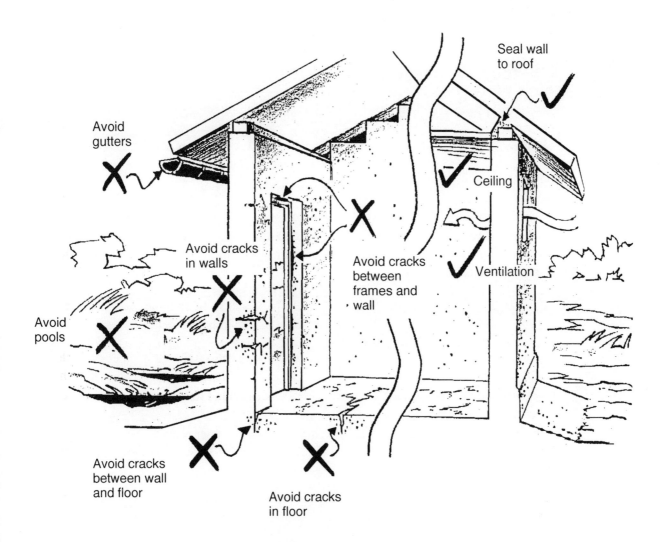

Walls, floors and health

Part G: Earthquake areas (areas of medium and high seismicity)

G1 RAMMED WALLS IN EARTHQUAKE AREAS

Guide

The earthquake map indicates regions in which earthquakes have regularly occurred in the past. This does not mean that other areas are known to be entirely safe from earthquakes. Unfortunately, an earthquake sufficient to cause damage to rammed earth structures could occur almost anywhere – but the risk is much lower than in the indicated zones of medium and high seismicity.

Earthquakes produce waves of ground movement which result in foundations being moved violently in both side-to-side and up-and-down directions.

For earthquakes larger than intensity V the tensile stresses introduced by these movements in masonry structures such as rammed earth are likely to cause cracking to occur. Nevertheless, a well-constructed building may well be able to withstand larger earthquakes safely, even after cracking occurs. The standard sets out the minimum requirements for safety.

Although tensile forces cannot be resisted by masonry structures such as rammed earth, recent studies in the USA have shown that classical 'elastic' theory is not a good guide in predicting how such structures will behave in an earthquake.

Tests at Stanford showed that before cracks have developed, high frequency effects dominate, but once cracking has started, then low frequency effects are stronger: the behaviour changes. The collapse of a wall or structure cannot be predicted from the time the first cracks appear; collapse will depend on:

o the absolute thickness of the wall, and its slenderness ratio;

o the degree of restraint at the top or sides;

o what added gravity loads are present (such as roof or upper walls).

Steel bars have been shown to bond well with soil, and will add tensile strength to structures otherwise weak in tension, thus giving added 'ductility' or 'stretchability' in earthquake conditions.

The following principles should be followed when building rammed earth walls in areas of medium or high seismicity:

Careful siting
Avoid sites where rock falls, landslides and tidal waves are possible.

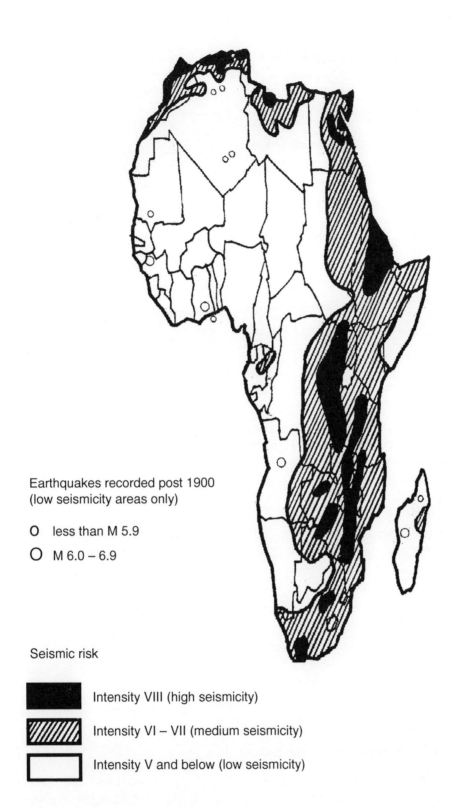

Earthquakes recorded post 1900
(low seismicity areas only)

O   less than M 5.9

O   M 6.0 – 6.9

Seismic risk

                        Intensity VIII (high seismicity)

                        Intensity VI – VII (medium seismicity)

                        Intensity V and below (low seismicity)

Maximum intensity – Mercalli scale
once in 50 years for average ground conditions

Areas of medium and high seismicity

G: EARTHQUAKE AREAS

Robust building form

Ideal shape is circular or square. Symmetry is important, so rectangles are less good than squares, but better than L-shapes. Avoid openings near corners, keep openings small and well-spaced. Connect each wall to a cross wall at frequent intervals. Add horizontal steel bars at corners, at points of weakness: window cill-height, lintel-height.

Lightweight roofs are preferable to heavy roofs.

Firm foundations

A solid base for earth walls is important. Brick, stone or concrete foundations up to ground floor level are preferred; in any case, footings should be stabilized using cement or lime (see A2). In earthquake areas rammed earth buildings should not be built on soft soils.

Strong vertical structure

Walls should be built up in such a way that joints between lengths of formwork do not line up vertically. 'L' moulds should be used at corners, and 'T' moulds used for bonding cross walls. E3 should be modified as shown in the standard following.

Distributed openings

Part E should be modified as shown in the standard following.

Secure non-structural items

Heavy non-structural objects such as stove pipes, chimneys and built-in furniture should be tied so as to prevent collapse in earthquakes. Adequate connection of door and window frames is important (see F2).

Safe modification

Care should be taken when extending existing buildings. Rammed earth should not be bonded to other materials. However, bonding new to old rammed earth is recommended.

Regular maintenance

All buildings need to be regularly maintained; in areas subject to earthquakes this is especially so. How much will depend on the original standard of building, but unstabilized earth structures will need to have maintained:

- the roof (to protect the walls from softening through leaks);

- cracked or spalling renders (to prevent damp penetration building up behind the cracks);

- failed damp-proof courses or wall-base protection (to prevent rising damp at wall base);

- physical damage to wall itself (to prevent the spread of damage by further wear and tear).

Rammed earth walls should be mended using the same materials as the original; otherwise there is a risk that the new will separate from the old.

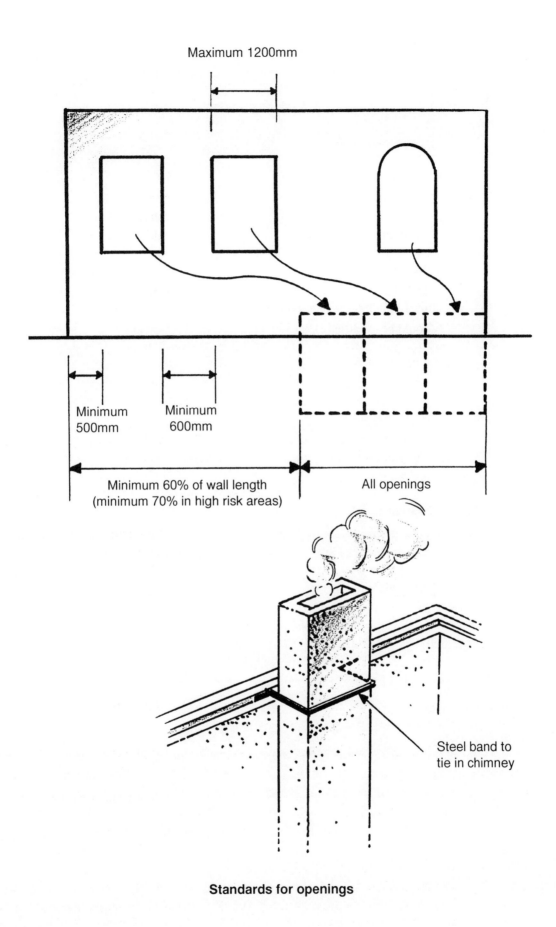

Maximum 1200mm

Minimum
500mm

Minimum
600mm

Minimum 60% of wall length
(minimum 70% in high risk areas)

All openings

Steel band to
tie in chimney

Standards for openings

G1: RAMMED WALLS IN EARTHQUAKE AREAS

Standard

Special consideration shall be given to the strength of rammed earth buildings in areas of medium or high seismicity, as defined in the map.

The principles set out in the guide shall be followed; consent must be obtained if this is not possible. In all cases, rammed earth buildings shall be no more than one storey high, unless supported by calculations passed by the building supervisor.

In all cases, buildings shall have a ring-beam on top of the wall which is continuous, strengthened at corners, tied to wall and tied to roof.

E2 (Openings) shall be modified as follows:

- o width of openings in any wall as a proportion of wall length shall not exceed:
  areas of medium seismicity: 40%
  areas of high seismicity: 30%
  and the maximum width of any opening shall be 1.2m;

- o there shall be a pier of minimum 500mm width between openings;

- o no openings shall be less than 450mm from the external angle of the wall;

- o where lintels are used, the bearing on the wall shall be at least 300mm.

E3 (Stability of walls) shall be modified as follows:

- o walls shall be built up in such a way that joints between lengths of formwork do not line up vertically;

- o walls shall be fully bonded to cross walls, and the length of wall between corners or buttress walls shall not be greater than the following:
  areas of medium seismicity: 15 times its thickness
  areas of high seismicity: 10 times its thickness;

- o the height of a wall from floor level shall not be greater than the following:
  areas of medium seismicity: 10 times its thickness
  areas of high seismicity: 8 times its thickness.

Deemed to satisfy ring-beams

Either:

timber; single ring-beam system in areas of medium seismicity (intensity VI - VII) and parallel beams in areas of high seismicity (intensity VIII). Timber to be minimum 100mm x 75mm cross-section, and protected from damp and insects, and be anchored to wall at maximum 600mm centres using not less than 8-gauge galvanized wire loops anchored minimum 450mm deep into the wall below (all as described in F2); roof members should also be fixed to ring-beam in all cases.

Or:

reinforced concrete (RC) ring-beam for areas of medium and high seismicity (intensity VI and above, see map) to be built minimum 255mm deep and to full width of the wall, having a minimum of four steel rods (not less than 0.8% of beam area in all) and hooped at minimum 300mm centres all round.

PART G: EARTHQUAKE AREAS

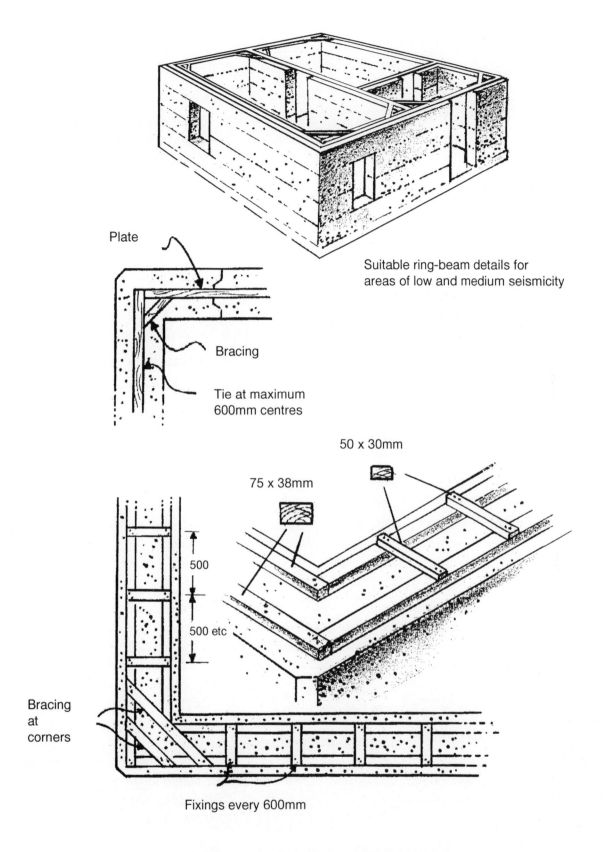

Plate

Bracing

Tie at maximum
600mm centres

Suitable ring-beam details for
areas of low and medium seismicity

50 x 30mm

75 x 38mm

500

500 etc

Bracing
at
corners

Fixings every 600mm

Building requirements in earthquake areas

G1: RAMMED WALLS IN EARTHQUAKE AREAS

Appendix 1

ACKNOWLEDGEMENTS

The Consultants are indebted to the help of people and institutions too numerous to mention. We also set out here sources of information and references used in preparing this code of practice. Special reference is made to help given by CRATerre which kindly opened its library to the team. No responsibility for data or advice is implied by the Consultants where use has been made of these sources, but thanks are given to all those workers in the field.

The illustrations to the code were prepared by Adam Brockbank, of 19 Davis Road, London.

References are given in full once only, and in short form thereafter.

Introduction

Various soil diagrams	Norton, John, *Soil Analysis for Building*, MUDH/REXCOOP/GRET, Paris (1989)
Use of hand auger	Fitzmaurice, Robert, *Handbook for Building Homes of Earth*, HUD, Washington DC
Rainfall in Africa	Spence, Robin, *Development Atlas, version 1.02*, Cambridge Architechtectural Research, and based on Bartholomew World Atlas (Peters projection)
Seismic risk in Africa	Spence, Robin, *Development Atlas, version 1.02*, Cambridge Architechtectural Research, and source: Munich Re (1978) & Swiss Re (1989) (Peters projection)
Lateritic soils	Charman, John, *Laterite in Road Pavements*, CIRIA Special Publication No. 47, London, (1988) and 'Tropical Residual Soils', *Quarterly Journal of Engineering Geology*, Vol. 23, No. 1 (1990) (Peters)

Part A: Materials

The soil tests	Norton, John, *Building with Earth: A handbook*, IT Publications, London, (1986) and *Soil Analysis for Building*
Water absorption	Okwero, Owino, *Co-op in African Region on Technologies and Standards*, UNCHS (Habitat) (1989)
Stabilization	Spence, Robin, *Building Materials in Developing Countries*, Wiley, UK (1983)

Part B: Formwork

General   Middleton, G., *Earth-wall construction*, Experimental Building Station, Canberra (1983)

Rammers   Fitzmaurice, Robert, *Manual on Stabilized Soil Construction for Housing*, UN Technical Assistance Program, New York (1958)

Horizontal formwork   Norton, John, *Building with Earth*

Vertical formwork   Keable, Rowland, *Australian Rammed Earth*, unpublished (1991)

Part C: Groundworks

Foundation table   *The Building Regulations*, approved document, 'Classification of sub-soils' (1990)

Floors   Stultz, Roland, *Appropriate Building Materials*, SKAT/IT/GATE (1988)

Termite resistant timbers   Usher and Ocloo, *Tropical Pests Bulletin 6*, Centre for Overseas Pest Research, ODA (1979)

Termite control   Logan, J. & Buckley, D., *Subterranean Termite Control in Buildings*, Royal Society of Chemistry, Vol 2, Issue 1 (1991)

Part D: Superstructure

Test cube   Norton, John, *Building with Earth*

Drip test   Norton, John, *Soil Analysis for Building*

Visual test   Okwero, Owino, *Co-op in African Regions* (Appendix)

Part E: Stability

Openings   Ghana Standards Association, *Ghana Building Code*, draft (1989)

Part F: Details and finishes

Surface treatments   Patty, Ralph, *Paints and Plasters for Rammed Earth Walls*, S. Dakota Agricultural Station, bulletin 336 (1940)

Part G: Earthquake areas

Seismic protection   Spence, Robin, *Building for Safety: Technical Guidelines*, draft, Cambridge Architectural Research (1992)

APPENDIX 1

Appendix 2

Conversion table for common units

Length

mm	metres	inches	feet
1	.001	.0394	.0033
1000	1	39.4	3.28
25.4	.025	1	.083
305	.305	12	1

Area

m^2	ft^2
1	10.76
.0929	1

Volume

litre	m^3	in^3	US gal	Imp gal	ft^3
1	10^{-3}	61.02	.264	.220	.0353
1000	1	6102	264	220	35.31
0164	1.6×10^{-5}	1	4.3×10^{-3}	3.6×10^{-3}	5.8×10^{-4}
3.785	3.8×10^{-3}	231.1	1	.833	.134
4.546	4.5×10^{-3}	277.4	1.201	1	.160
28.32	.0283	1728	7.47	6.23	1

Mass

gramme	kg	tonne	lb	ton
1	.001	10^{-6}	2.2×10^{-3}	9.8×10^{-7}
1000	1	.001	2.205	9.8×10^{-4}
10^6	1000	1	2205	.984
453.6	.4536	4.6×10^{-4}	1	4.5×10^{-4}
10^6	1016	1.016	2240	1

Force

Newton	kN	t	lbf	ton
1	.001	1×10^{-4}	.225	1×10^{-4}
1000	1	.102	225	.100
9807	9.807	1	2205	.984
4.448	.004	4.5×10^{-4}	1	4.5×10^{-4}
9964	9.964	1.016	2240	1